EMPOWERED MINDS

Transform your mind

Expand your consciousness

Live a life of purpose

Kalí Alfaro

PSYCHOLOGIST

Cover Design by 100Covers.com
Interior Design by FormattedBooks.com

ISBN 978-0-6489393-0-6 (paperback)
ISBN 978-0-6489393-1-3 (ebook)
ISBN 978-0-6489393-2-0 (audiobook)

As a thank you to my readers I'm offering a free hypnotic meditation to support your empowerment journey.

https://alfapsychology.com/product/
empowered-minds-resources/

On this page, you will find a hypnotic meditation you can access to support your healing and empowerment journey. Your password is IAmEmPOweReD!

CONTENTS

FOREWORD

My wife Judy and I met Kalí Alfaro near the end of August in 2015. She was in Colorado to attend a week-long trauma education workshop with a therapist who works near us. I conduct experiential shamanic therapy sessions from our home, and Kalí had three of those sessions. She also spent whatever spare time she had during that week meditating in our Medicine Wheel, as well as having several lengthy conversations with us. She enjoyed being in our serene mountain retreat and, although we only had that one week, she remains in our hearts forever.

Kalí is compassionate, sensitive, kind, generous, creative, and she is a totally present human being. You will certainly be aware of this as you meet her in the pages of *EMPOWERED MINDS*.

As she remains in our hearts, she may also remain in yours. She also remains in the heart of Pachamama (Mother Earth) for what she does not only for individuals' lives, but also for all the animals and plants whose lives she touches. Kalí has made and continues to make this planet a better place. She is persuasive in her invitation that we do the same thing. She makes that possible as she guides us on the path of "healing, connecting and shining."

In this book Kalí points out the fact that when we become more authentic individuals, we absolutely affect the planet. She calls this "the ripple effect". She also goes to great lengths to explain how we can accomplish this and lead lives full of bliss instead of ones filled with fear and anger.

Kalí writes from the depth of her soul and tells the story of her own life. The pain and difficulties she experienced became the ground for discoveries that led to her own healing. The creative way Kalí lives has also served her well in making a "plus" for the planet. She shows us how to follow a more effortless path through life ourselves, and she ends every chapter with exercises to understand, broaden, and incorporate into our own lives what we read. What Kalí writes puts us in a state of virtual reality. With her wide perspective she takes us all the way from learning about the science of brain biochemistry to experiencing the blissful effects of shamanistic ritual.

Kalí writes in her book,

> "I want you to know that I value every little experience I have had. I have finally crafted a loving and fulfilling life. Best of all, my mind is my best friend, a safe and wonderful space to be in. Nature is always by my side (and) I feel I have a mutual love affair with life, supporting and caring for one another."

I have written,

> "I believe we incarnate for two reasons – to learn how to work a physical body and how to take care of a planet.

The two are intertwined. If I'm observing and tuning my physical body, I'm also taking care of the planet."*

Kali's way of living is a wonderful example of these intertwined reasons and that's what she now teaches. May the ripple effect she sets in motion take you forward in your own life.

Jack Stucki, Subtle Energy pioneer
*("*Healing Magic,*" WINNpost.org, August 7, 2020)

This book is dedicated to Pachamama, Mother Earth.

To Pachamama, thank you for holding me through every breath
Thank you for inspiring me with your beauty and your greatness
The mountains that have held my feet
The oceans that have embraced my joy
The forests that inspired my imagination
The night sky that fills me with mysticism
I thank you.

ACKNOWLEDGEMENTS

My beloved parents Ethel and Umberto who instilled unconditional love in my heart and mind, you have given me the best gift in this world. Thank you for being my parents and holding me with so much care. I will always eternally love you. My brother Kamal who is my ever-present friend, support, and inspiration, I love you. My uncle Armando who is my second father, your love, support, and wise advice is carried in my heart wherever I go. Every single person in my family has had a loving and significant impact in my life, I honor you and I thank you. You are my tribe and it is a delight to be part of your tribe. My friends around the world who have loved, encouraged, and supported me every step of the way, I love you. You are the family I have chosen; thank you for your loyal friendships.

I'd like to acknowledge all the family and friends that have taken the time to listen to my visions, have participated in the analysis of this book and have guided me with their wisdom. A special thanks to Lucia Velasquez for her guidance in all matters of lexicon.

I'd like to acknowledge Dr Rick Collingwood who trained me in hypnosis and shaped my skillset. Deanna Forster who has been a source of inspiration in all matters of the heart, nature, and the mind. Lisa Schwarz for showing me how interconnected and profound therapy can be. Jack Stucki for taking me to other realms and expanding my vision on life and love. My many mentors and people who have significantly influenced my life and work, I thank you. To all my patients who have shown me what true courage looks like. You turn up time and time again to heal your wounds, face your demons, and rise to your potential. Your vulnerability, strength, and dedication to improving yourself are constant sources of inspiration to me. Thank you for letting me share your stories of courage.

A special thanks to the animal kingdom; you have shaped significant parts of my life. Your essence has shown me the true meaning of embodied spirit, unconditional love, play, and freedom.

To all the wild women who dare to be themselves and walk to the rhythm of your own beat, I am with you.

INTRODUCTION

Expansion, New Mexico, 2019

I felt my heart expanding with such intensity that it no longer felt inside my body, my feeling was no longer confined to my physical being. I felt I was everything, everywhere and nothing at all simultaneously as I sensed bliss running through my cells. My mind was aware but it wasn't aware; I was aware of my body feeling a blissful, serene, and ecstatic sensation and, at the same time, I felt my mind off in the atmosphere in another realm. I was so connected to the universe, life, everything, yet I was totally disconnected from the reality I had known. My body was totally relaxed; I felt extreme love, love that I could sense vibrating in my cells.

A love so powerful it enveloped me in a warm cocoon of comforting light, it seeped into my pores, loving all wounds I carried into healing. As I felt this loving energy, it contained my body and my heart; it made my body gently shake. It had a nourishing quality and a sense of freedom. I trusted the experience, I surrendered and let go. I let go of trying to understand what was happening and dissolved into it. Bliss can't even begin to describe this sensation. This loving energy held me as I expanded so far, so vastly that it was like an otherworldly expansion. It had no beginning or end; I was aware of so many things at the same time but I was also in no particular place. It was as if I were floating and moving but felt that my body was on the chair. I felt my body dissolve into particles in the sky way up in the atmosphere, yet my physical body was shaking with the vibration of bliss running through it.

When I heard a voice instructing us to return to our bodies and the present moment, I became more aware of my physical body. I now felt aware in several places simultaneously. My consciousness had expanded so far out that it felt like going out into space and calling all those tiny particles that make up "ME" back home into my body. I returned back to full consciousness after some time. I was shaking gently, I felt such deep love and clarity, it was like I'd been in a dream state. The most amazing dream state and now I regained awareness returning to the perception of reality I was familiar with.

I came back relaxed, sharp, and with an increased sense of awareness. It felt as if every sensation had been magnified but I felt weightless. My day unfolded in wonderful ways, and I was able to feel a deep sense of connectedness to myself, others, and life itself. It felt incredible; it stayed with me and grew as I embodied and integrated this experience into my day. I was more present and loving in my interactions with others, less bothered by things that would normally irritate me. I felt like I'd had an upgrade, my body felt more alive, more revitalized, and vibrant. I had an influx of ideas, thoughts and concepts.

I walked outside and sat in front of the mountain range on a cold crisp day and wrote ideas down. There was such a sharp clarity to my thoughts that I was able to express them effortlessly and clearly. My words just flowed out of me; it was as if I were observing myself writing. This may sound like a drug induced trip or a lucid dream of sorts, but it was neither. It was an experience I had during a meditation I experienced while on a neuroscience conference/retreat in New Mexico with 1,200 other people. It is also an experience I have regularly, sometimes daily, as a powerful side effect of meditation and self-hypnosis. I feel more alive than I ever have; I feel more sharp, productive, and present than I ever have.

Bliss is available to everyone, flow is available to everyone, and feeling a sense of expansion and unconditional love is also available to everyone. It's easy to feel these experiences at significant moments in your life when something external of great significance unfolds. Sometimes, you feel an incredible sense of connectedness in the midst of an amazing natural setting after climbing a mountain. You may feel it while deeply immersed in the middle of an art project. It's also possible to experience these sensations daily, without any need of external events unfolding. Diving into the beautiful depths of your mind will open the door to this immense sense of love, bliss, connectedness.

I have dedicated a large part of my life to going around the globe and learning from the best in multiple fields of healing. I have learned some of the most ancient techniques of accessing the subconscious mind. I've studied healing techniques to improve performance, activate optimal well-being, and lead a balanced life. I have learned from some of the world's foremost experts in dealing with trauma, illness, and all matters of the heart. Most importantly, these experiences have shown me the way to heal, empower, and live a life filled with purpose. They inform the treatments I carry out with my patients, the retreats I run for large groups, and how to live my own life.

I have seen people transform in the most inspiring ways. I have witnessed people go from feeling panic and fear daily to living their best lives, feeling happy even when things aren't perfect, reaching higher levels of self-love and self-acceptance, and overcoming illness and chronic pain. People's minds have transformed, changing their entire perspectives on life to make life not only work for them but to feel life is worth living, fully. I have observed my own transformation. I want to share how I have done this, how so many others have done this, and how you can begin to do this.

On this journey, I will guide you to accessing your mind's deepest realms. I will show you how to reduce negative thought patterns, worry, and fear. I will educate you on how toxic stress is for your body and what you can do about it. I will share my own journey of healing and how this has helped me and my work. I will show you how to best use your mind with real clinical case studies. I will give you exercises that will shape your mind and open your heart.

I share these very personal stories with you to give you an idea of the life circumstances I was born into. These circumstances created trauma in my brain, dysfunction in my life, and a sense of suffering. I was drowning in a dark abyss of disconnect and was gravely unwell. More importantly, I share these experiences with you to show you that I have overcome these life traumas. I healed my brain and the hurt I carried. I did this in natural ways, in loving empowering ways. My passion and deepest desire is for you to do the same.

I will share some techniques used in clinical case studies to inspire you to heal and demonstrate the ability to change and evolve. All identities used in case studies have been modified to preserve the privacy of individuals.

I want to share my most sacred learnings from the past two decades of my soul searching and career.

My aim is to empower you for your own good but also for our good. If you are more empowered, you'll create more inspired communities. Your own change will motivate people and this will be positively infectious. The more empowered, loving, and courageous communities are the greater our world will be. I have a big vision and you're part of it.

Keep trying. Keep working through your stuff and keep showing up to your life with an open heart and mind. If you don't try, you can't win. Show up to life willing to be better than you were yesterday. Show up willing to listen instead of talk. Show up willing to be vulnerable instead of defending your point of view. Show up to every page, every chapter, and every exercise with a willingness to learn, improve, and implement changes.

This book is for people who are willing to take full responsibility for their life, transform their minds, and tackle their challenges, all in the name of empowerment. It's for people who are dedicated to exploring themselves, who have a desire to be better and do all they can to get there. This book is for people looking for something more in life, a greater sense of purpose, more connection, more love. It's a book that will push your buttons and challenge your perspectives so you can move forward and be your best.

This is a journey that had an ugly messy start, a challenging middle, and a beautiful present moment. I welcome you to join me on the adventures and techniques that created my mind today. If I can do it, so can you!

Today, I shall write words that turn into magic.
Dreams that unfold as I think them.
Today, my words create my reality spontaneously.
I activate a magnetism that attracts only life's
sweetest nectar into my life, effortlessly and
gracefully, for my highest good and the good of all.
Today is a truly magical day, I welcome miracles and
joyous surprises to visit me often and lovingly.
I beam love onto the World.
Today is a magical day

Kalí

CHAPTER 1

MY SOUL EVOLVES

My little soul chose a special place to enter this world: Chile, a land of magnificent beauty with the Andes mountains as its spine and clear blue skies. It's the birthplace of some of the greatest poets, wines, music, and people, a place of contrasts with arid deserts in the north and glaciers in the south. Imposing volcanoes and pristine lakes scatter along the long skinny terrain. The ever-present Pacific Ocean with deep blue waters nourishes the coast. Chile is a cultural hub; every street corner has a guitarist, a poet, a mural, and a hopeless romantic begging his lover to return. The smell of delicious food awakens the senses, magnetically bringing people together.

Two different families came together to ensure my arrival. From my mother's side, came a migrant Jewish family with Eastern European heritage. My father's side was a Western European Catholic family. There is Romanian, Russian, Spanish, and Italian blood in my body. The essences of these cultures are embedded in my DNA: the strong Italian sense of family gathering around long tables with home-cooked meals; the music and songs of ancient traditions that graced my ears; and intergenerational living that warmed my heart and filled the home with loving family.

Chile has a turbulent past, and I came along in the heart of its eighteen-year Pinochet dictatorship. I was born in Santiago, Chile at the start of winter on a crisp June evening at 1:40am. It was a cold, rainy night; there was a military-imposed curfew that cautioned my parents as they drove to the hospital to give birth to me. I was born to my beautiful healthy Jewish mother, received by my charismatic loving father. I quickly made my way out into the world, happy, healthy, and well. I was brought up in a normal middle-class family in the city. My family members were caring, present, and affectionate. My life revolved around our relatives; we were a big joyful community. My grandparents lived with my parents, my brother, and I for some time and I was always surrounded by a lot of warm people who would often squeeze my cheeks. The presence of food, family gatherings, and cheerful music were common visitors in my life. I am lucky to have been graced by the presence of loving relatives from all sides of the family.

Although it was in the middle of the dictatorship, we had some freedom. We could go play at the park down the road or go to the store a few doors down, and we felt happy and free. We would often go to my aunt and uncle's nearby farm. We'd sit on rocks covered in bright green moss, eating hot bread in front of the fire. It was nestled in a valley between two magnificent mountain ranges. The Andes on one side and the coastal mountain range on the other side. I remember the smoky smell of leaves burning on the fire. We'd run around exploring and pick up rocks and sticks. We'd pick leaves to make lemon balm tea on the fire. The days there seemed magical, all of us together, playing, exploring, eating. There was a beautiful sense of family and joy. These moments exploring in nature created strong bonds to the Earth for me. I remember long sleeps in the back of the car after a whole day out in nature. I was happy, and, for the most part, this was a wonderful time for me.

In 1987, things got more challenging for Chile and my parents. They decided to migrate from Chile to Australia. This was one of the most heart-breaking experiences I was to ever go through. I was taken away from everything dear to me: all the people I loved, our neighborhood, the language, the hugs my grandparents gave me. Even the sweetness in the air that was instilled in my DNA, that was about to be taken away too. I didn't understand why we needed to leave; I didn't want to leave. I only knew that it was a very long trip to the other side of the world. We left, and I was inconsolable.

We arrived in Australia in February, which meant heat, real desert wind heat that we had never experienced before! My mom would roll up wet towels and put them in the fridge, then she'd tuck the cold towel bundles under our necks to cool us down. We were definitely not use to this. I had to start a new school, learn a new language, and make friends. I didn't know anyone other than my immediate family. Needless to say, it was damn right daunting. So, I began to do the only thing I knew that would comfort me, eat. I began to eat my way through my feelings, my uncertainty, my fear, my sadness, my disconnect. I started to build layers of fatty protection around my little body.

When I was at school, I felt disconnected, lonely, and scared. I was the new kid who didn't know the language. I just wanted to go home. My dad's brother and his children were living in Perth; that's why we ended up in Australia. They were our blood relatives, but we'd never met them. So, it felt exciting, distant, strange, and new. My parents began to fight at home. It was just the four of us, and it felt small. The house felt tense and lonely without my extended family. My mother had to learn how to cook, speak a new language, adapt to a new culture, and manage the family as well. It was far from easy. I saw a lot of tears and witnessed a lot of arguments. It felt like my happy bubble had painfully burst in my face. My mom had her first bout of cancer within the first year of arrival. This devastated her; she felt isolated and wanted to be around her family in Chile and her familiar surroundings.

We didn't last long the first year. By the time Christmas came around, my mom grabbed us and we were on a plane back to Chile, leaving my dad behind. I didn't understand what was happening. All I knew was that it was painful and we were moving again. My feelings were so mixed; I was so sad to leave my dad. He was my world, my rock, my protector. Yet I was so excited to go see my family back in Chile. Unbeknownst to me, this was going to be pattern for us for the next ten years. Moving back and forth from Australia to Chile, from school to school, house to house. All my external stability was gone.

My mom began to struggle; my parent's marriage slowly crumbled. All those things that once made me feel happy, loved, and safe were scattered all over the world. I didn't know who I was or where I belonged. I had an ocean of feelings I couldn't express, so I repressed them with food.

My mother's mental health began to deteriorate rapidly. A once happy, beautiful, comfortable woman was now a stressed, sad, and worried woman. Tears would often run down her face, and I felt sad and helpless. She started to slide down this black hole of despair. Every time she'd disappear into depression, I desperately hoped that she'd come back to us. I hoped so deeply, I prayed so faithfully that she'd stay. But she wouldn't, or couldn't and didn't. She'd always slip away into the deep dark abyss of depression, sadness, and hopelessness. My mother was in and out of hospital for depression;

this was part of our norm. A norm I don't wish upon anyone, but I sadly know it's a reality for many. So, our life continued and we carried our scars and our joys as best we could. My parents did their best, they always provided for us and loved us. But life hit them hard, and pieces of them had gotten lost along the way.

Art had entered our lives to provide a bit of sunshine. My father had gone through art therapy after a horrendous car accident, and he had recovered wonderfully, reinventing himself as a sculptor. My mother was also beginning to make art a part of her life and healing. I witnessed snippets of peace and creativity in the middle of their struggles. Precious seeds of hope and inspiration were being planted in my little brain. Some of these moments filled my heart with hope and joy.

Art was lovely, but, nonetheless, life seemed hard; it was filled with struggles and hardship. By the time I graduated, I had been to seventeen schools, had lived in several countries, and had no idea who I was. I was overweight, felt disconnected, depressed, and damn right angry with life. We were all over the place, fragmented, frazzled, and disconnected. I didn't understand how this happened when our beginning was so united, loved-filled, and tight. I felt I was spinning and didn't know which direction to head into. My family were now scattered in different countries. I was caring for my mother and struggling to figure my life out. In the midst of all this in 2001, my beloved aunt committed suicide. This rocked our family to the core, and life was a huge mess. My central nervous system was well and truly shaken up. My view of life was pretty dark; I felt attacked by life from all angles. This impacted many of my life choices. At first, I ran away from mental health as fast as I could.

I gravitated toward art, design, and creativity. I didn't have anything to give to others. I felt depleted, tired, and heavy from the experiences I'd had. Art had supported my dad's healing tremendously, so it seemed right. I felt art was my pathway. I felt it was a language that allowed me to express through shape, form, and colors. It had its own magic. I felt inspired, and this was a healing experience for me.

I felt I was beginning to process and express parts of my soul that had felt dormant for so long. There hadn't been the stillness required for creative expression to even peep through the cracks. I had been in survival mode for so long. I allowed myself the process of exploring the world through art. My mind was now focused on color, design, and shapes. I was able to look at life through the lens of beauty. Maybe this allowed my traumatized child part to come to the surface and play with colors once again.

I enrolled in an arts degree at University. I lost myself in photography labs. Obsessed with developing the next film, the anticipation of the images coming to life in front of my eyes. I thought it was magical. The photography darkrooms where timeless spaces. There was no room for distraction or worry, it was pure creative energy. I'd slip into flow states, endless hours of focused creativity seemed to have created a sense of connectedness for me. It filled me with excitement like nothing else had until that point. I felt alive to be able to express and tell a story through images. I could capture mood with light, a person's character with their gaze, it was mesmerizing to me. I began to feel inspired; I'd finally found a language that allowed me to express myself without words. The pictures spoke for themselves.

I felt my life was beginning to unfold in more peaceful and beautiful ways. I began to feel a spark of life rise within me. I learned the importance of creative expression for healing. This began to form a strong identity within me, to creatively express. I realized creativity was part of our family's healing journey, and

I embraced it. I slowly made my way into psychology studies and began to weave my love for art and the mind together.

In the midst of dealing with life and the traumas we were experiencing, there'd be moments of contemplation. In these moments of peaceful contemplation, sometimes, I'd have out of body experiences I couldn't quite understand. It was a sensation of feeling here but not quite present, a deep sense of love and connectedness to all. Everything made sense to me temporarily. These moments were definitive for me as they connected me to a feeling of expansion, an experience that there are much grander things that we may not quite understand with our minds. These moments were like little nuggets of gold, like magic dust sprinkled over my existence. They were less frequent than I'd like but they gave me meaningful experiences. These experiences would pique my curiosity. They would gently nudge me to remind me of a grander plan. This was nice, but let's be real; I had to deal with "real" life, and that was far from fun, magical, or exciting. I'd slip back into struggling disconnected mode. I spent several years fluctuating from illness to wellness.

As the years went by, life unfolded in mysterious ways. I landed in the hands of a hypnotherapist in my early twenties. This was one of the most transformative and defining moments of my life. This would guide me, shape me to becoming the woman I am now. The power of deep transformation was unknown to me at the time. Through hypnotherapy I experienced results that I had been wanting for years in regular therapy but hadn't achieved. I started to feel sensations in my body that I didn't know were possible such as bliss, contentment, and peace of mind. I started to transform in the most magical ways, my mind started to mold into something more. I began to shed the extra weight; I started to release my limiting beliefs. I felt my inner spark and vitality coming back.

More importantly, I was beginning to feel that these feelings weren't just fleeting sensations. They would stay with me, creating deep subconscious changes within me that were palpable. I was greatly impressed and inspired. So, I threw myself into learning hypnosis while completing the final year of my undergraduate psychology degree. I developed a deep curiosity; I felt aligned with my soul purpose. I felt excited to understand how to work in the subconscious mind; it was finally what I had been looking for. I began to see the mind was so much more powerful than the limited view of using a tiny percentage of your brain power. I began to experience states of being truly unlimited. It sparked curiosity and a thirst for learning. I was now experiencing deeper and more profound depths of consciousness, states of consciousness no University textbook ever spoke about. I wanted to be the type of therapist who would facilitate true transformation.

I began to understand that I was not my family history, I was not my story, and I really wasn't anything I didn't want to be. But it required more than not wanting to be something to transform it. I was clearly psychologically scarred from a series of events in my life. These events had created negative belief systems. I was so moved by the first hypnosis experiences I'd had, that I committed to healing. I was determined to transform my brain into the most amazing space. I chose to heal my wounds, my trauma, my fears, and all the emotional baggage I was carrying that was affecting my life. I realized I needed to take responsibility for my mind. I decided to eventually turn my life and brain around; it was a deep dive into the subconscious.

I was so curious about different healing modalities, that I made it my mission to explore. I began what was to be a decade-long journey of discovery. I dedicated my time to learn about some the most mysterious techniques from around the world. I traveled to small, remote villages to speak to elders. I hiked up mountains to visit sacred sites of the Incas. I walked along the Sahara Desert to meet Berber tribes. I sat in endless ceremonies of sacred rituals. I attended the most cutting-edge neuroscience conferences. I sat for hours on end in silent meditation retreats. I read books on the mind, healing, and humanity. I sat in forests listening to the trees. I flew across the world to lie on crystal beds designed by scientists. I chanted with hundreds of strangers. Sat in ancient temples at the foot of the Himalayas. I drank bitter herbal remedies given to me as offerings. Visited shamans who blew smoke into my face and chanted strange mantras. I studied regressions and practiced them with colleagues. I drove into majestic valleys in the Andes mountains of Chile where I experienced miracles and mysterious happenings. I spent endless days meditating with monks in the Cambodian jungle. I spent time in the Australian outback in traditional ceremonies. I had awakened a thirst for rich experiences. I walked alongside blind elephants, raised orphaned kangaroos, and felt whole again. I did everything I could to become the person I now knew I could be, any version of me that I decided to be.

I want you to know that I value every little experience I have had. I don't wish that my life had been any different. I believe everything I went through shaped me and guided me into the person I am now. I feel only love toward the traumatic experiences and people involved in them. I hold so much love for my family, every single one of them. They have been my rocks and guiding stars in ways they are not even aware of. I utterly love life. I believe my love for life has something to do with forgiving and loving every aspect of it: the good, the bad, the ugly. I loved and let go of my past, I openly welcome my future, and I live in the present. I realized I could create my healing, write my story. I continue to do so every day.

Along the way, I met wonderful people, mentors, healers, and great thinkers. I began to realize life is truly beautiful. It is full of brilliant people willing to give, support, and collaborate with one another. It has filled me with hope that we are indeed creating a magnificent place to live. Wonderful people will inspire you and fill you with hope; surround yourself with great people.

I now run my own psychology business, hypnosis retreats, hypnotic meditations, and I continue to fly around the world to keep learning from the best. I consider myself to be healthy, happy, and I'm surrounded by wonderful people. I have finally crafted a loving and fulfilling life. Best of all, my mind is my best friend, a safe and wonderful space to be in. I have my magic formula; I know who I am and what I need. I prioritize exercise, meditation, good nutrition, and good company. I make sure I feel inspired and make time for creativity and stillness. Nature is always by my side. I still have challenges and struggles; I have good days and bad days. Most importantly, I feel empowered to deal with all that life throws at me. I know it will hurt at times; I know it will be uncomfortable and frustrating. I also know you are never stuck in the midst of the storm for too long. The sun always shines on you, and you gracefully pick yourself back up and continue. I feel I have a mutual love affair with life, supporting and caring for one another. I've let go of socially imposed pressures. I've broken away from the shackles of other people's expectations of me. I've created my own path, true to my essence. I feel comfortable in my own skin and finally feel safe to be me.

My passion is to help my readers, my patients, my community, and all my loved ones to be able to do what I did and so much more. I want to empower you to heal from trauma and step up to being your best self. This book will take you on some of my most memorable and adventurous journeys. It will provide you with an understanding of how your mind works. I will guide you with exercises I have specifically and lovingly created for you. All in the hope that you too will create an empowered mind. My desire is that you will feel you have the tools necessary to heal your wounds and connect to yourself, life, and others. Finally, I hope you allow yourself to shine; only you have the power to do this, to live a life that truly represents your magnificent luminous essence.

From the most beautiful depths of my heart, I thank you and accompany you on your journey. May you feel the love I hold for humanity in every chapter and story I share. May you feel the passion in the adventures, the deep reverence I hold for nature. I honor all of you actively working through your "stuff." May you end up believing as I do that the idea of infinite possibilities is at your fingertips.

You are like a night sky filled with sparkling ideas.
As fiery as an outback fire,
As vast as the ocean.
Your spirit is divinely connected to all life.
Your imagination is your greatest friend,
Imagine wonderful things as they will unfold.

Kalí

CHAPTER 2

MATTERS OF THE MIND

Valle Sagrado, Shamanic Expedition Peru 2018

As I hiked through el Valle Sagrado, 2,800 meters above sea level, I could see the world around me, accompanied by the majestic curves of the Andes mountains, each step taking me further and higher up the cordillera, breathing in thin, cold mountain air. I observed old ruins around me and Inca women drying potatoes and weaving fabrics. We were getting closer and closer to the next sacred site where the rituals would be performed. In the distance, you could see endless snow-capped mountains. Green pastures were all around us with wildlife in abundance. Eagles soared up above and alpacas grazed around us. We finally arrived at the Temple of the moon. This is where the Incas would honor and worship the moon's divine energy. They were guided by astrological phases for the planting and harvesting of their crops. As we sat in a circle honoring this site, silence was our companion. You could feel and listen to the unspoken knowledge held in the Earth, the rocks, the birds flying above. We took some time to just connect to the land and allow our minds to settle into our bodies. As our shamans Don Humberto and his son performed the sacred offerings to Pachamama. They blessed us one by one with coca leaves.

We were encouraged to think about our ancestors, the present moment, and the future. When Don Humberto talked about the future, he wasn't referring to a five-year plan or even a ten-year plan. He was talking about future generations. Not just your grandchildren but future generations we'd never witness in this lifetime. How could we act now in a way that would have a positive impact on Pachamama's future 50,000 years from now. This was a whole new level of future planning. I must admit that this was novel to me. I liked it and embraced it. It made me feel humble and honored to carry a bigger vision. It gave me a sense of responsibility. The idea of a distant future I would never see was to guide my life and my work today. It allowed my mind to expand and connect to a greater vision. This idea of a greater vision embodies Eagle medicine. In shamanism, Eagle medicine represents Christ consciousness, Oneness. This challenged my thinking and reframed my role. I was being asked to be an Earth keeper, a custodian, conscious creator of all the tomorrows. I was being asked to be aware that my actions today will impact the future.

How can you embody a vision of life that is greater than your current situation? How can you be aware that what you do today will impact the lives of many others years from now? How can you rise from the ground away from limitation of what you can see just in front of you, fly high as the Eagle soars through the skies and see the whole picture, see how one river affects a valley kilometers away, how that valley affects the next, how everything is connected? Every action has an impact on everything else; ultimately, we are all one. This challenges belief systems, ideas and thoughts we have been raised with. It was a novel way of thinking for me. It gave me a sense of honor for what had come before me. It left me with a profound sense of responsibility. It reminded me to act mindfully, to be cautious of my actions, knowing they will impact the future. So, I ask you to challenge your beliefs. How can you alter your consciousness to be aware, mindful, and conscious of your actions? How can you have a positive impact on the world today for all our tomorrows 50,000 years from now.

How Your Mind Works

One of the most common stories I hear as a psychologist is "it happened out of nowhere." People say this when they've had an anxiety attack, rage, or bout of sadness. Although, at the time, it may seem like it came out of nowhere, the reality is that we are walking fields of memories. We carry ancestral knowledge, beliefs, emotions all lying dormant beneath the surface. The Earth around us carries stories and experiences within it also. It is all energy encoded with stories. You may be triggered by a smell, sound, thought, song, or someone's resemblance, sometimes, even by a dream you had that seemed real and vivid. Your mind is constantly making meaning of the world around you. You carry so much more than what you can see with your eyes. You will eventually see that everything is interconnected deep within you and all around you.

Your mind is such a valuable part of you; it is important that you understand how it works. You must think of it as the most valuable asset in your life. When you have a strong, healthy, happy mindset, your life will represent these things also. It is valuable to invest in creating the mindset you desire. Your mindset can be volatile if untrained, fluctuating from light to darkness. These fluctuations can occur as a response to thought patterns, external circumstances, people, and experiences. At other times, it will seem to come out of nowhere. These experiences that feel like they're coming out of nowhere are programs triggered in your subconscious mind. They poke their little heads out in times when you get triggered, whether it's obvious or not. Like an untrained animal, peaceful and gentle at first, it'll defend, attack, run, howl, or act in unpredictable ways (if triggered, survival instincts will kick in). The untrained mind is very similar.

How is it that you can fluctuate from a state of well-being to a state of utter despair? You are walking fields of memories and experiences. You are constantly engaging with aspects of your mind and with the external environment. There is a relationship constantly unfolding in the background. You have thousands of thoughts each day, pulling up emotions, memories, and ideas. At times, you'll be triggered and flip into undesirable states, often giving rise to deep seated emotions. The untrained mind will be easily triggered; it will react and dwell on these unpleasant feelings. When you carry many emotions, traumatic experiences, and hurt that have not been dealt with, it won't take much to trigger you. You'll take things personally, dwell on and ruminate over things, and look for things to be upset about. It's not all your fault. You see, the mind is responding to the orders you're giving it; you're just not aware of it.

Your mind is a beautiful instrument, always responding to your every command. Your mind will do what you tell it to do, so it's important that you become aware of what is going on in the background. The pure nature of engaging with life will allow you to have experiences that you will give meaning to. Your perception of these experiences will partially depend upon what you focus on and how you interpret those experiences. This is important to understand, as it will shape your experience. You have programs in your subconscious awareness that will guide you to focus on certain things. This will shape the idea of who you are and what your life is. If you focus on all the bad things in the world, see the awful things on the news, speak to people about it, reinforce the view of "the world is awful," you will indeed have an experience of the world being awful. Your brain is doing its job; you're constantly giving your brain orders. You've told it to look for awful things, and it's following these instructions. Similarly, if you're suddenly in the market to buy a new car, imagine you've decided on a red Suzuki Vitara. You'll suddenly start to notice there are red Suzuki Vitaras everywhere on the street. It's not that now there are suddenly more red cars; you've just told your mind to focus on that, and so it does. These signals are being given all the time in the mind. Let's explore how some of this works. I want you to assess the subconscious programs that are running you so you can work on improving them. How does your mind get programmed? How can you begin to work on creating more empowering, healthier programs in your mind? How can you create optimal levels of well-being and functioning? These are the types of questions to be asking yourself.

How Is Your Mind Programmed?

Your subconscious mind begins to be programmed from the moment of conception all the way up until seven years approximately. A child's brain is primarily fluctuating between alpha and theta brain waves during this time. These brain waves are when learning is absorbed most easily, beliefs are formed, and information is readily integrated. Theta is the brainwave activated during hypnosis; it is one of the most conducive to suggestibility, imagination, and learning. Think about your early years as a dream-like state of super learning and absorbing everything in your mind, similar to hypnosis. Children are downloading everything that is happening around them and absorbing like a sponge. All comments, experiences, interpretations, and meanings are downloaded without much thought. Everything that happens to you gets downloaded as a truth or belief system. Your critical analytical mind is not yet developed; this means you don't have the ability to analyze or discern. You haven't developed your ability to understand the context in which events unfold.

The first seven years of a person's life can be very significant, it can determine the type of programs you create. This is why childhood memories can often be so defining. Early childhood experiences can have such a significant impact upon your well-being. Parents, teachers, and early life experiences have a big role to play, shaping the quality of little minds. You create programs based on your experiences of the world around you. These programs get installed in your subconscious mind. You are mostly unaware of them, until they begin to pan out into your life through your behaviors and life choices. Once the mind has embedded these programs, you begin to play them out automatically. The mind's role is to play these programs out and prove that the programs are right. Your mind will look for situations that will reinforce the program you carry.

Imagine this: A child puts his hand up to answer a question in class, he gets it wrong, classmates make fun of him and call him stupid. There will be a rush of emotions: shame, fear, nervousness, self-consciousness, anger, and sadness. These emotions will secrete a cocktail of chemicals. This happens whenever you feel a really strong emotional reaction to something. These strong reactions filled with emotions create changes in your brain and make neuro-associations. This is essentially an association of an event to a feeling that has now been "branded" in your brain. This child may develop the neuro-association of "asking a question = being stupid." The brain interprets this as a direct download and turns it into a belief, "I'm stupid." This will be installed in the child's mind.

The child may develop the program of "I'm stupid." Depending on his personality, environmental factors, and so on, it may play out in a certain way. For example, he might turn into the class clown. He might put himself in situations where he is being "stupid" and made fun of. He might be an under achiever and think, *I won't bother since I'm stupid anyways,* and not try at all in class. He may be an overachiever, get fantastic grades, accomplish magnificent things, but deep inside never feel smart enough. As you can see, these programs play out their role of proving they are right in different ways.

These programs essentially run you until you start to really work on them. Many people walk around, unaware they have subconscious programs dictating their lives. Some of these programs and beliefs are rarely detected until life starts becoming problematic. A good way of noticing if you have limiting beliefs is by observing patterns in your life. There might be a pattern of always being abandoned by others, constant illness, or never feeling good enough. Observe what areas of your life you feel you are repeating patterns; this will give you a good idea of some of the internal beliefs you have installed. People generally don't pay attention until something is broken or gone. Someone may not notice they have the program of "I'm stupid" until either a friend or partner may point it out to them. They might be told, "Have you noticed that no matter how much you achieve you always feel that you're not smart enough?"

The programs you have in your subconscious mind play a significant role in your well-being. Approximately 95% of your programs have been downloaded in your subconscious mind approximately by the age of seven. You think you are an adult running the show, but, really, it's your child brain running the show. Learning continues as you develop; after seven, you turn to habituation, learning by repetition until you form a habit. In your formative years in school, most of the programs have been installed; the subconscious mind is in the driving seat. Buckle up! Most of your programs are already set by the time you reach adulthood. The way you engage with your programs can either reinforce or weaken them. How you engage with your subconscious mind is the key. Your primary way of engaging with the programs in your mind is through questions.

The quality of your life depends of the quality of questions you ask. This is an idea shared by many of the worlds' great thinkers. Questions activate mechanisms in your mind that will search for answers within your own "library" of knowledge. This library of knowledge has been built over time based on the experiences you've had. Let's explore this a little further.

The Reticular Activating System (RAS) is the brain's sorting and searching machine. The RAS is the ultimate analyst for all the questions you throw at it. It sorts information into the following categories: Dangerous, Important, Pleasurable, and Interesting (DIPI). Your senses sort the information, and it is categorized. When assessing a situation, you look for signs that will provide you with the right information. If you are crossing the road, you look around, you assess the distance of a car, the speed at which the car is traveling, the distance you need to cross and how quickly you can move along that distance. This process activates questions. You ask, is it safe to cross? Are there any sounds that are alarming? All this is being examined in your mind as you think, feel, and act.

The RAS then searches for answers to the questions you ask it. In the story above about the program of "I'm stupid," you might ask, "Why can't I ever get it right?" "What's wrong with me?" Your mind will find an answer, and if it can't find a factual one, it will revert to your programs and tell you, "Because you're stupid!" The mind will always turn to what's most familiar, even if that's negative. This is why you need to challenge your belief systems and programs in your mind. They were developed when you were a little child, and you didn't have the ability to discern. The impact of the questions you ask yourself daily have a significant role in the experience of your life. What questions are you asking yourself regularly? What types of programs in your subconscious mind are you accessing regularly? You can begin to interject the process and change the way you are by changing the types of questions you ask yourself.

The mind will always find an answer, even if it needs to attack you and call you stupid. All it's doing is going on the programs you already have; it's doing its job. The answers generate feelings; poor questions lead to negative feelings. Disappointment, anger, despair, and shame may rise if you feel you can't ever get anything right. This creates the secretion of chemicals in your body that will lead to either action or inaction. When you're feeling disappointed, you're more likely to sit there and dwell on it. When you dwell, you let the floodgates open with chemical secretions. As a result, your association to that belief system will grow stronger, reinforcing that neural pathway. This will then lead to a self-fulfilling prophecy; you will be overwhelmed by the chemical effects of the negative emotions. When you are overwhelmed, you are experiencing a chemical storm. If you do this often enough, it will turn into rumination, excessive worry, anxiety, and depressive symptoms. This is then experienced in your body by emotions and physical sensations. Feelings such as fear, anger, disappointment will activate your central nervous system (CNS) and set off your alarm system into fight, flight, or freeze. This is a survival stress response. When you are in survival mode, you are stagnating, stuck; there is no room for growth in this state. This is not a time for creativity; your mind is not thinking about what would be the best question to ask. You are stuck in a downward spiral of negative thinking and flooding the body with chemicals that will prepare you to defend and counterattack, avoid, or freeze.

Questions will ultimately create feelings, feelings create a chemical change in your body, these chemicals will either drive you toward GROWTH or STAGNATION. The chemicals created by your feelings have significant impacts upon your body. They will either energize you or deplete you. You very rarely see a depressed person walking down the street fully energized. Similarly, you rarely see a happy person walking with their head held down, slouched, and lethargic. Your emotions fuel your behaviors, they will activate health and vitality or illness and lethargy (Lipton, 2016). You want to be aware of how you're fueling your body and begin to take charge of that. What if you were to ask a different question to challenge the program of "I'm stupid"? Imagine you caught yourself moping. I know you might not mope, but humor me for a minute. You go down that rabbit hole of despair and disappointment, then you interrupt yourself. You stop yourself in your tracks. You remember to ask an empowered question. Maybe you ask, "How can I do this differently?" Now that's a great question; this activates the RAS in your brain, and you begin to search for answers that won't attack you but lead to problem solving. You see, "why" questions will throw you down a rabbit hole.

"How" and "what" questions will activate your problem-solving capacities. So, your brain may come up with a bunch of ideas such as: "Ask your friend Ben to explain it to you," "Maybe I can try using a different textbook that explains it more clearly," or

"Maybe I'll make an appointment with my lecturer and ask for help." The possibilities are endless. The importance here is that the brain has activated a problem-solving mechanism. Instead of dwelling, consumed by emotions that paralyze you, you begin to take charge. You now feel more in control of the situation. When you feel more in control, you begin to feel more empowered. By feeling empowered, you get motivated, and it seems more plausible that you will find a solution. This gives you hope and allows you to feel more confident in moving forward. This option has a different chemical reaction that will flood your body with energizing chemicals. It will literally "feel" good. When you feel good, you think better, get more creative, and step into proactivity.

Sometimes, asking a different type of question is all it takes. Nothing external has changed at the time you ask the question; the pure fact that you asked a more empowering question has changed you. That is powerful. Just think about it for a second. You can ask a different question and change the chemical makeup of your body. That's powerful! You have interrupted the neuropathway of the negative thinking that reinforces the belief system of "I am stupid." By doing this, you are weakening that pathway in your brain. Even if it's for a moment, interrupting negative thinking weakens that pathway. You want to constantly interrupt negative thoughts until you completely weaken that pathway. It's like thoughts are cars in traffic, you have just put a road block. Then you have activated a different set of questions that have created different emotions and chemical reactions in your body. This process begins to recruit parts of the brain that activate novel thinking. The more you do this, the greater your ability to create a new belief system. New thought patterns give you a sense of hope, control, and direction. These feelings allow you to focus on solving the problem rather than dwelling on it. This literally fuels your body to take action.

You make that phone call, you send that email, you go to the library and look for other books on the topic. Here, the intention is to solve the problem; you have given your mind a command to go find the solution.

Remember that your mind obeys your orders, it's following your instructions. Your mind is both very simple and extremely complex. You need to be aware and understand how you're functioning. Then you can train and create empowering states, feelings, or situations. You begin to have greater awareness and control of who you are. When you become aware you can choose better options, choice is freedom.

Thought/question	Answer	Feeling/Emotion	Behavior
Why can't I ever get it right?	Because you're stupid	Disappointment, anger, frustration, hopelessness	Paralyzed by negative thoughts
What textbook can I find that will explain it more clearly?	Good idea, I'll go to library	Empowered, in control, hopeful	Energized to go to library

It's important that you begin to realize you can change your state of mind and your feelings by asking a different question. Nothing outside of you needs to change at first; just focus on your internal environment. The interesting thing here is that by changing how you think, you are likely to change your external environment also. By allowing yourself to ask about a different book, you allow yourself to feel more in control and empowered. This may lead you to go to the library and you might see a friend or even bump into your lecturer; the possibilities that could unfold to your benefit are many. You are open to opportunities. A change of focus fueled your body to move in a different direction. You may end up at the library with a friend who is having the same issue and has a great book recommendation. You may have a social catch up afterwards and feel a sense of being understood, that everyone is going through a similar experience. This makes it normalized; you start feeling that you're not stupid after all.

By sharing how you feel, you allow yourself to be vulnerable, to be human, to be seen. When you share your feelings, you give others permission to do the same. This allows you both to have a shared experience; you bond. Bonding increases a sense of belonging, which is important in your development. A sense of belonging allows you to feel safer; when you feel safer, you activate calmer brain waves. Calmer brain waves are conducive to better learning. All of this comes together. Now you begin to feel more capable of figuring things out, more supported. You have an experience of starting a problem-solving journey that allows you to feel more confident of solving problems. When you start to feel more confident, you soon start to act more confidently. Confident people are magnetic, clear, and happy. Feeling confident is a strong emotional experience, this will secrete 'feel good" chemicals. You have the power to change your life experience by changing the questions you ask yourself.

When you have strong emotional experiences, you start rewiring your brain. There are thousands of questions you ask yourseif each day, all day long. These questions engage with the library of beliefs in your subconscious programs. It takes dedication and awareness to continuously interrupt your thought patterns. Like anything new, the more you do it, the better you'll get. The investment results in an immediate reward (positive feeling). The long-term reward is the construction of positive feelings and patterns. You are constructing empowering patterns right now for a more magnificent future.

If all of this feels too foreign right now, I want you to think about it in a slightly different way. Think about the following questions that might help you:

- If you weren't feeling "stupid," "stuck," or "overwhelmed," how would your life be?
- What kinds of things would you be doing?
- What would you do differently?
- How would you engage with people differently?
- How would your self-talk change?
- What kinds of people would you surround yourself with?
- What talents would you share with others?

These questions will hopefully lead to thinking about experiences that begin to shape your world. There are so many different ways of changing your mind, your thoughts, your situations. I want you to start thinking about how you can begin to change right now, even if it's simply that same question: "How can I begin to change right now?" Give yourself permission to play in life in general but also with these ideas. Allow yourself to not take things too seriously, especially your thoughts. Play with them; be a bit silly, more light-hearted. It's good for the soul. You are not defined by your thoughts, but you can be controlled by them. Start creating more empowered questions and thought patterns today.

**Interrupting your thoughts with
empowering questions is the key!**

When you begin to understand that what you think has such a significant impact upon your life, you really start to respect your mind. You pay attention and take note of what's unfolding in the background. Equally important is to understand that what you say has as big an impact. The way you speak to yourself and to others is possibly one of the most powerful tools you have. You can promise the world with your words; you can break hearts and start wars. Words are powerful; they carry frequencies, meaning, and vibration. Begin to be truly aware of what you say. Think about this problem-solving journey as an expedition where you get to know yourself better in every aspect. By becoming more aware of who you are, what you are thinking, and how you are speaking, you can regain control of your mind again.

Self-awareness is such a wonderful thing; it is where all change begins. The very moment you become aware you have a choice, you have great power, so choose wisely. Let's quickly go back to your subconscious mind first as it relates directly to your thoughts and words. The subconscious mind is a very literal place. The subconscious mind takes everything literally. When you say, "I am angry," you are affirming that your identity is that of anger. The mind won't decipher if you feel angry or if you are angry. It will simply take it literally. The more you use the words "I am," the stronger your subconscious is getting a command to create.

The use of I AM statements form part of your identity; your mind will do whatever it takes to make sure it does its job well. I'm, by no means, the first person to mention the importance of "I AM" statements; this goes back to antiquity, mentioned in scriptures, in the Bible, and in the writings of many of our greatest thinkers. Whenever you start a sentence with "I AM," you are, indeed, making a powerful statement directly linked to your identity. It is of absolute importance for you to become aware of what you are linking your identity to. If you say, "I am sad," you're indeed affirming that your identity holds the feelings and concepts of sadness. Your mind takes that quite seriously. It makes sure you are indeed thinking, feeling, and acting sad. This is very different than saying, "I feel sad." Stating that you FEEL sad is simply a feeling statement; it does not define you and it is not who you ARE. You are always creating, so be aware of this powerful tool and use it consciously. The wise Florence Scovel Shinn said, "Your word is your wand" (Scovel Shinn, 1989). I know this may seem a little too simple, but it has incredible power. The way you speak to yourself will lay the foundation of how you communicate. It has power not only in the way you are with yourself but also impacts greatly on the way you engage with others.

How you express your feelings with others has significant effects. For example, if you had an argument with your partner and you say to them, "I am sad because you did XYZ," what you're saying is that they created an identity of sadness within you. If you believe they can do that, you are no longer in control of how you feel and who you are. You have given your power away. You are at the mercy of life and what people say or do or don't say or do to you. It's subtle, but very important. In contrast, if you were to say, "I feel so sad that you said that to me," there is an important difference. First of all, you are owning your feeling. Saying, "I feel sad" is just you acknowledging your feeling. A feeling state is not a permanent state, so your brain knows that this is a momentary experience. It is just a statement of a sensation; it does not link to who you are. I invite you to notice how you talk to yourself, how you express your feelings. That's your first step; be self-aware.

Proverbs 15:4 "Gentle words bring life and health; a deceitful tongue crushes the spirit."

CASE STUDY: Katie's words

Katie is a fifteen-year-old girl who developed severe anxiety and depression around school issues. She'd developed a school avoidance phobia. She'd been badly bullied in her previous school, unable to overcome fear and ruminating thoughts. She was hyperaware of anything anyone said and was on edge in survival mode constantly. I got the full story of what had happened, all the awful things she went through, the relentless verbal abuse she experienced, her body shutting down. I knew she was experiencing trauma in her CNS. She presented as a sweet young girl who truly wanted to overcome her fears. Katie knew she didn't want to continue to avoid school or any other situation for that matter. She struggled to learn; her brain had shut down and gone into survival mode, so there was no room for learning. Other people's words had destroyed her, had made her feel unsafe, on edge. She started doubting herself and spiralled down into severe anxiety and panic attacks. That was her body's way of saying, "STOP, this is too scary!" Her body shut down; she couldn't think straight and perform at school. This made her think that maybe some of those mean things people said were true. The meaning she gave the bully's words were so strong that it started changing her biochemistry. It started to create a state of depression and hyperalert CNS, resulting in anxiety, vomiting, and shaking. Unfortunately, she had some abandonment issues. Her dad had left when she was an infant. She'd overheard some nasty arguments and name calling as a young child. The bullying was triggering old belief patterns in her subconscious mind. They had absolutely nothing to do with who she actually is, but were just belief systems created in early childhood. She had been in the middle of her parents' arguments, absorbing every bit of them. She was reacting to the past as if it were happening in the present. Her mind couldn't decipher if she were in danger or safe but ruminating. So, the body behaved as if it were in danger all the time. Her ruminating thoughts were signaling her brain to be in survival mode. In an environment where she felt afraid, she'd momentarily forgotten who she was. Her biology took over, and she was drowning in hormones of stress that had clouded her true self.

We started to play with the idea of constructing a new life, a new ideal of how she wanted to feel. Through this activity of self-exploration, Katie realized she was limiting herself. She was so stuck in fear and survival, the best she could come up with was feeling "calm" or "content" at school. She struggled to come up with ideas of what she wanted her future to be like. She was so paralyzed by fear, that calm and content was as far as she could go. I worked with Katie on releasing these fears and ruminating thoughts. My aim was to get her out of survival mode. After a couple of sessions, she began to feel safer. Now she was ready to create a better future. She was ready to grow. We explored how she would like to feel if there were no limitation, no block. What would that reality look like for her? I encouraged Katie to think of the most amazing feelings imaginable to her. She lit up, her eyes grew wide, she smiled, looked at me in disbelief, and asked, "Anything?" I replied, "Yes, anything, anything at all. Go wild, and when you think it's big enough, go bigger.". She started to say words like excited, inspired, amazing, outstanding, joyous, "totally myself." Katie started to construct a new picture of what her ideal was. It was like she'd allowed herself to remember what her true essence was before it had been crushed by a bully's words. We started to peel away the layers of fears, release the negative thinking, and teach her how to feel safe in her body again.

We started a beautiful journey, working toward creating her ideal self. We had a beautiful conversation one day. I said to her, "Look, people will call you names, say mean things, crush your dreams, and limit your talents; you don't need to do it to yourself. Let's look at creating something so amazing in your mind, so strong, that no external person could ever crush it. This is your unique vision and its yours to play with." Katie felt she had permission to feel "good" again. To be a child, to be creative and her amazing self.

It's important to assess what meaning you give to words and how taking others' comments too seriously can harm you. Realize that you need to be your own best friend, your most encouraging coach, and your kindest self. In a safe space like a therapy room, Katie was able to learn and soak in the information. She was able to express her fears and have them dissolve with her mind's powerful imagination. She felt a big black heavy ball of pressure lying on her chest. The ball wouldn't go away; it would paralyze her and make her feel tired and scared, as if it were warning her all the time. I used her mind's creative powers to dissolve that black ball of energy. I guided her into a magical hot spring in nature, the mist coming out of her pores represented fear. She allowed the ball to dissolve as the warm water held her safely and nourishingly (resembles the womb). Her favorite spirit animal was an eagle, so I had brought the eagle in. The eagle hovered over her, whispering encouraging words as she let go of this fear. She released this sensation she had been holding onto or as she felt IT was holding onto her. So, we used the mind's language to slowly dissolve her fears. I then got her to begin to reconstruct the idea of who she was. To dream big, see her own truth. I got her to imagine what her life would feel like if she felt safe at school again. So, then we started to really work on developing this true self. She made it stronger, more amazing, more resilient. She made sure she was able to shrug off any negativity or mean comments from others. She was building a new reality for herself, based on the original framework of who she was before the bullying, and making it bigger.

It was as if we were scaffolding the house and renovating the inside, putting in strong structures that would endure in difficult moments. Katie was a delight to work with; she had tears and anxiety at first, and then she allowed herself to shine. What a beautiful privilege this is to observe transformation right in front of your eyes. She began to shine like you wouldn't believe, she began to feel so confident and invincible that her entire demeanor changed. She was no longer a victim of her past experiences. Katie was beginning to master the most beautiful emotions, creating empowering belief systems. She crafted an improved version of herself. Every time she visualized her true essence, she was flooding her body with the right chemicals. This reinforced a strong belief system in her brain. The more she felt these emotions of joy and confidence the stronger her self-belief became. Katie returned to school, she made good friends, her performance improved, and she was able to feel happy again. She felt confident enough to deal with life, stress, and nasty comments. She worked hard on constructing a strong self-esteem, and she began to flourish.

Train Your Mind

One very important factor here is that you need to train yourself to be a certain way. You want to create the neurological pathways in your brain that will strengthen a strong healthy sense of self. The more you practice in a safe environment, the more the brain begins to embed this as part of your makeup. Practice in your home, in your office, when you're exercising, etc. The key here is to train yourself daily. Remember that you learn through repetition and habituation. It's important to do it daily, as this prepares you for when you need it. The more deeply embedded this is within your mind, the easier it will be to access in challenging times when you really need it.

It's a little bit like asking me to run 10kms right now. I might struggle. If I train and start running 1km every day, then 2kms the next week, I start to get fitter. Then the following week I run 5kms twice a week. After a few weeks of training, I will most likely be able to run 10kms easy. Your mind and brain are very similar to training your body. It's about building the internal strength and resilience so that when I do actually *need* to run, I can. Similarly, if you practice feeling confident and safe at school or work, you will most likely feel that way when you are there. You have made it familiar in your mind. Your mind will take you toward what feels most familiar. Even if familiar is toxic!

Psychological skills need to be embedded, revisited, strengthened, and practiced over and over so they become second nature. Daily practice is so crucial. It takes constant and consistent effort to create new coping skills. Each day, you can construct an even better foundation for the next day, building bit by bit. Know that every effort, every action you take with the right intentions, creates a better experience *now* for an empowered tomorrow. Plants seeds of empowered mindset, water them daily, and watch them grow.

Before you go any further, I would like to encourage you, strongly and lovingly, that you practice being kind to yourself during this process. Any change of any kind requires a lot of head and heart space. Please let yourself be your best friend, the most loving, encouraging, and supportive friend. Do this because you know you are worthy; you deserve to feel comfortable in your mind. At the end of the day, you are the one who has to live in your mind. You are the one who carries the feelings you have daily. You are the one creating the circumstances in your life. Allow yourself the privilege of being your own best friend.

Clean Up Your Mess!

In order to become your own best friend, you need to do a bit of cleaning up. You need to heal and deal with some of the hurts and demons you carry, right? How do you heal your traumas and hurts from your past? I think it's important to acknowledge that everyone has something to deal with. Whether you've had a "perfect" life or not, everyone has "stuff" to work on. Most people have issues with attachment, self-worth, abandonment, and rejection. Fear resides as an unwanted visitor in the back of most people's minds. This creates a sense of not being enough: not good enough, not attractive enough, not smart enough, not wealthy enough, etc. This sense of not being enough creates a sense of disconnect. Not feeling heard, seen, and validated are common themes in most cultures and populations.

Now that you have a little bit of an idea of how to create empowered thoughts, you need to deal with the deep wounds underneath all that. It's important to acknowledge you are not alone; we're all in this together. When you begin to explore the issues you carry or the challenges you face, being kind to yourself is crucial. No point trying to improve yourself if you're going to beat yourself up in the process, right? Your thoughts, feeling, and behaviors basically make up who you are. Thoughts create a feeling; feelings fuel your behaviors. You have a thought: "I hate how I look," "I'm disgusting," or "Why can't I get anything right?" That thought creates a feeling like anger, sadness, frustration, or disgust. That feeling fuels the behavior you act out in road rage, snapping easily, withdrawing from others and dwelling in your sadness, eating your way through feelings of disgust, and so on.

Your behavior is powerful; it's the unspoken language that you use to express yourself. Behaviors are fueled by the chemicals secreted by your feelings. Behaviors are difficult to change if you're addicted to the chemicals you secrete. You become addicted to these chemicals because it's who you are! You identify with them it's part of you. Remember, the mind likes familiarity, so it will stick with what's most familiar. The mind goes with what's most familiar, as it feels "safe," even if that is feeling depressed. You see, it might not feel good to feel depressed, but it's known. The unknown is scary to the mind. This is why it's sometimes hard to change. You'd rather stick with what's bad but familiar than try something new.

How Does That Feel?

Let's explore feelings a little bit. Guys, don't run, this applies to you also. If you feel angry, you will have cortisol and adrenalin running through your body. This creates a frantic energy field, it will make you on edge, defensive, and aggressive. You are on the "look out" for danger or to defend yourself, constantly feeling attacked. When you're having feelings of disgust, you feel uneasy and heavy in your body. When you're feeling depressed, you feel lethargic and heavy. The body dislikes unpleasant states, it will instruct you to avoid, repress, distract. The tricky thing is that if you're wired to feel anxious or angry all the time and the body dislikes this, you'll get stuck in a habit of activating that state and then repressing it. This creates internal conflict and puts you out of whack.

One of the quickest ways of getting out of this is unpleasant state is by activating the pleasure center in your brain. The pleasure center in your brain is most easily activated by consuming food, alcohol, and drugs. The consumption of external substances overrides the chemicals of "bad" feelings with endorphins. By doing this, you disconnect from the unpleasant feelings and engage with the sensation of pleasure. This then distracts you from the uncomfortable feelings. It may be a quick fix; our society is full of quick fixes. Unfortunately, quick fixes don't lead to pretty outcomes. Generally, after the effects of the substance have worn off, those feelings you were trying to ignore come back to bite you. It damages you in the long run. It reinforces the feelings you were trying to avoid in the first place (anger/disgust/sadness). It gets you addicted to that substance (food, alcohol, drugs). You want to connect to your feelings not disconnect from them. Even if it doesn't feel great, your aim is to connect to your feelings; this is the only way you'll be able to process them. By connecting to them, you are paying them the attention they deserve. When you do this, you are opening up to the opportunity of healing. Part of this journey is having the courage to sit with the uncomfortable states within you. When you do that, you can face them, challenge them, and eventually heal them. Sitting with these feelings does not mean ruminating, worrying, and becoming overwhelmed. It means acknowledging they're there and then working through them, creating more empowered thought patterns that become familiar so you override the limiting patterns.

When you are feeling joyful, the brain secretes hormones that will energize you. You will feel motivated to do things; you're more productive, loving, and healthy. You're more likely to exercise, finish a project, or be open to going out with friends socializing. These behaviors lead to GROWTH. You want to be consciously flooding the body with chemicals that make you feel good. Joy secretes dopamine and serotonin, neurotransmitters in the brain. These chemicals allow you to engage with your outer world more positively. Essentially, you want to make sure they're your friends and that you see them often. They're feel good chemicals. They not only make you feel good but also boost your immune system, improve your cognitive abilities, and make you feel more alive (Pert, 1997).

The change in your biology fuels your behaviors. In simplistic terms, emotions will either STRESS you or make you GROW. Your brain literally changes as a result of the emotions and experiences you have. You absolutely want to increase the emotions and experiences that increase well-being. You can change your body, your feelings, and your life by creating an empowered mind.

You want to have two main goals when you are looking deep within:

1. Increase the frequency of the emotions that are conducive to GROWTH (joy, excitement, gratitude, love, peace, awe, inspiration).
2. Decrease emotions that induce STRESS (fear, anger, resentment, guilt, shame, sadness).

- Identify what activities, places, and people activate strong emotions.
- Write them down and get to know yourself better.
- Wherever possible, avoid people, places, and experiences that induce stress.
- If you can't avoid hostile situations, dedicate time to working on releasing the negative emotions these environments may trigger. Dedicate even more time to creating a stronger internal environment so the external circumstances have less of an impact on you.

Your aim is to consciously seek out experiences that create positive emotions. Your intention is focused on your well-being and growth. In order to grow you must feel calm. This is why it's so important to create more positive experiences in your life; it literally changes you. You want to tell your central nervous system (CNS) that you are safe. If you are safe, you can grow and create. One of the fastest and easiest ways of grounding and calming your nervous system down is by closing your eyes and deep breathing. Closing your eyes and breathing deeply allows the nervous system to slow down. You move from "fight or flight" sympathetic nervous system to "rest and restore" parasympathetic nervous system. By doing this, you begin to train your body to slow down, to stop producing stress hormones. You allow yourself to feel safe and grounded in your body. Feeling safe and grounded in your body is paramount for an empowered mind. It creates the chemical environment in your body for healing. When you do this, you begin to create a much deeper, more connected relationship with your own body. Most people have negative and destructive relationships with themselves and their bodies. They focus on them when they are sick, broken, or their body is not doing what they want it to do. How you relate to your body is crucial to your mental and physical well-being. Stressing your body out will lead to a sick, broken body and mind.

What a lot of people fail to understand is the fact that stress kills. When you are running around all day, stressed out, worrying, you are damaging your body. When you are stressed, all the nonvital functions of the body slow down or stop. Your digestive system, the repair of tissues and muscles, and your immune system are affected (Segerstrom et al., 2004). It's not important to digest your lunch when you are in danger; it won't "save" you. Stress means serious business; it means survival. This means that the nonvital functions in your body have to do their job when you've stopped stressing. For most people, it can only be done at nighttime when they've gone to sleep and are out of the way. Now they begin to sleep but wake up feeling tired, as the body has been working overtime. In the long term, this leads to chronic diseases, inflammation, and burnout.

If reading this is making you stressed out, STOP and take three deep breaths… Now continue.

Your body is a beautiful, highly adaptive piece of machinery. It's luxurious and wonderful; it has all the features you want, but it also needs to be looked after. Stress puts your mind and your body under great pressure, this is not fun for anyone. It's not sustainable for the body to be pumping such high levels of stress hormones without respite. Your body's stress mechanism was designed to be activated in response to a survival threat. After the threat is over, your body goes back to normal levels (homeostasis). In cavemen times, the threat was a tiger, for example. It was in your best interest to think of the worst-case scenario at that time. It increased your chances of survival if you thought about dealing with more than one tiger. The threat activated your fight or flight response. Your blood gets pumped to your extremities so you can fight or run. Your heart rate increases, your pupils dilate, your breathing changes. After the threat is over, there is a period of exhaustion, you rest, then you go back to normal. It's a wonderful system designed to get you out of danger.

Nowadays, the perceived threats are not tigers; they are emails, deadlines, financial stress, in-laws, ex-partner. Perceived threats create the same response in your body as actual life-threatening dangers. This creates stress; when you are stressed, you're afraid. When you're in fear all the time, your existence seems chaotic. Your body is designed is to be in homeostasis (balanced, chilled out, safe, and calm). This is its natural state.

The trouble is that we have so many perceived "dangers" in today's life that this protective mechanism is constantly being activated. As a result, the world is seeing huge amounts of diseases, illnesses, and dysfunction in people. Your mind starts predicting the future and preparing for worst-case scenarios. This may have been a functional protective mechanism in the past. Nowadays, this often turns into dwelling, ruminating, and constantly worrying about things. Being grounded and present with yourself and in your body allows you to be here in the present moment. If you are in the present moment, there is no room for worry. Diaphragmatic breathing (belly breathing) calms your CNS and allows you to be present. Deep belly breaths push on your vagus nerve, activating the secretion of the neurotransmitter acetylcholine, and stimulates the parasympathetic nervous system. This calms your whole body right down. There is science behind the age-old notion of "just take a deep breath" (McCall, 2007). Breathing deeply can be a powerful way to communicate with your body to stop some of those negative thought patterns getting out of control.

All of this talk about stress is important. Stress activates fear, and when you're afraid, you just won't function well. Figuring out how to deal with your feelings is a big deal. First things first, you must feel safe. Calming yourself down is an important step. When you feel calmer and more relaxed, you can think clearly and see things with a greater perspective. You also start getting in control of your body by actively calming down; this is a great coping mechanism. When you start controlling your nervous system instead of it controlling you, you begin to change your behaviors. By changing your behaviors positively, you allow healing to occur.

What Are You Doing?

There are several ways of engaging with the Universe and life. One of the most powerful ways is through your behaviors. Your behaviors represent you. You can use your behaviors to create circumstances in your life and to change your internal environment. Let's explore how your behaviors can do this. Imagine you wake up tired and don't want to face the day; you feel unattractive and a bit low. You lovingly force yourself to get out of bed, you make a hot nourishing breakfast and cup of tea, hot shower, and get ready. You put on your best clothes and make extra effort into doing yourself up. You crank up the radio and play your favorite song. You head out the door and you're already feeling better. You're more likely to actually get extra positive attention. A colleague may notice and give you a compliment. By doing this, you have changed the way life has engaged with you. This positive action will yield more positive results than the alternative. The alternative is feeling sorry for yourself, throwing on whatever clothes you can find, grab a donut, do your hair in the car, and hope no one notices how miserable you look and feel. You might get to work, and, instead of a compliment, your colleague might ask if you're okay. Behaviors emit a vibe, have a frequency, and can change you. Notice what kind of energy you're putting out to the world. Then observe how life responds to you.

Get into the habit of breaking through bad days; change your vibe and behavior. Create better days, push away the moodiness, the irritability. Put on happy music; take some deep breaths. Remember that this will create a chemical reaction in your brain that will reinforce your sense of being on top of it. It will make you feel more in control and confident.

When you become mindful of your actions, you begin to notice patterns in your life. You start to create an intentional relationship with life. Your behavior can be a powerful tool to create change. Sometimes when your internal environment (thoughts, feelings, mood) is not great, it's hard to snap out of it. It's not always easy to interrupt your thoughts patterns. Sometimes, it takes an action like getting up and going for a walk to interrupt the pattern.

A guided meditation or simply doing some stretching to upbeat music can help. It's important to use all your senses when challenging your thought patterns. It's easy to get stuck and lost in your mind, and it's sometimes challenging to interrupt thought with thought. You are a multisensory being, and those senses are there to serve you for your own healing and evolution. Think about how you behave and how this makes you feel. Now think about how your behavior creates a response from others. The more you observe yourself, the more you will understand that you are actively creating scenarios in your life. You are creating feelings and responses around you. When you become self-aware, you step out of autopilot. You start creating something different to change how you feel. By doing something new, your brain has to pay attention. When the brain processes information that is novel, it begins to recruit different parts of the brain that work together. These parts lay dormant when you are on autopilot. When you recruit different parts of the brain, you are learning. If your brain is more active by learning, it is a healthier brain.

A healthier brain is a happier brain. It's important to do new things, learn new things, and seek out new experiences. It wakes up the brain and gets you thinking, keeps you young and mentally fit. Remember, you want to grow; that includes growing new connections in your brain. You want to try new things so they create a more positive feeling. When you try new things, you don't feel life is so mundane. You're keeping it spiced up.

- What is one thing you could do differently right now that would make you feel better?
- A happy song, a walk, a funny video, a nice cup of tea, painting, meditating

- Do something right now, put the book down and shake your bones or have a stretch.

Please go for walks, daily if you can. Most people walk around like a zombie, unaware; they don't stop and smell the roses. When you do stop and literally smell the roses, you begin to notice more. The smell, the shape, the colors, the textures. You might even notice it long enough to see a bee landing on it. You might start thinking about the life of bees and how they pollinate plants. That might lead you to contemplate how bees have a direct impact upon your food production. You might even feel gratitude in that moment for realizing the massive role bees play in your own existence. Suddenly you feel grateful. You have created a whole new sense of connection to this entire scenario unfolding in front of you. Can you see that just by going for a walk to snap out of a mood, life gave you gratitude. Isn't that beautiful? Walking opens your mind, expands your heart, and offers you possibilities.

Use your behaviors to take charge of your life. Decide who you want to be and how you are going to prepare yourself. Prepare yourself knowing there are stresses in life, internal and external. It's very similar to having a good stretching warm-up session prior to a soccer game or physical activity. You're actively preparing yourself, knowing you will place your body under stress. The same goes for the mind; you begin to realize there is a whole bunch of things out there in the world that will get you off kilter. So, you prepare yourself. You act differently. Find out what feels good. Go for a walk, meditate, hit a punching bag, dance, paint, have a bath. Do whatever it takes to release stress and activate calmness. Visualize the wonderful feelings you desire more of. Creating strong daily habits sets you up for the day. Daily walks can be one of the most powerful activities. Walking lowers your stress levels, clears your mind, boosts your mood, and improves your health. You can use this time to notice nature, listen to affirmations or simply be present. If for whatever reason, you can't go for a walk, spend some time in the fresh air outside and feel your body in nature. If the positive effects of walking could be crushed up and put into a pill, it would be the world's best seller! Walk, my dear friend, walk!

Go With The Flow

If you choose to relate to your body in a more conscious manner, you begin to create a greater sense of harmony. You begin to feel a greater sense of control, and then you begin to flow more easily. When you feel you can flow easily, you'll notice you start to create a more harmonious environment within, more harmony in your mind, feelings, and body. You open up more lovingly and life will unfold in different, more magnificent ways for you. When this begins to happen, you then begin to realize the Universe actually does support you. You become aware you are in charge of your life. You are constantly creating, and your focus and perception are nourishing. When you are calmer in yourself, you can face the world calm and poised. Creating from this space allows you to face the world with this easeful energy. You begin to go with the flow, more open to opportunities, less hung up on things. Life has a magical way of allowing things to work out for you with a calm energy. You begin to feel better about yourself; you engage in life more courageously and openly. You start to flow more easily with the rhythm of life. These changes begin to happen as a result of the relationship you have with yourself. When you notice this, you start to value yourself more and make time for you. Make space and time to create a calm internal state of harmony within you. When you lovingly go inward, a deep empowering sense of yourself is awakened. You can start by learning to be calm in your body. Connect to yourself lovingly. Some people find this challenging. Like most things, you practice and keep doing it until it feels different, good different. This is a journey of self-discovery; go explore.

People often spend a lot of time in their heads, imagining things, going over scenarios. If it's negative, it's classified as rumination. Ruminations will send signals to your brain, secrete hormones of stress, stagnate, and paralyze you. By now, you've also learned that when you do the opposite, you have an amazing outcome. Let's look at how targeted visualizations can create a new mindset, change your brain, and essentially create a much better life. Hypnosis is just that!

Hypnosis, What Is It & How It Works

Hypnosis is a natural, altered state of consciousness using words to deliberately create and facilitate desired change in another (Ludwig et al., 1965). Hypnosis uses the brain's imagining faculties, engaging images along with specific words and suggestions to create changes. This can be very healing and powerful when applied by a health professional in a safe and ethical manner. Hypnosis has historically been used for many reasons, including hypnotic anaesthesia in surgical procedures. In the 1800s, surgeon James Braid operated on hundreds of cases using only mesmerism and hypnotic anaesthesia. It is a true testament of the power of the mind. In hypnosis, the person is aware mentally of what is going on but the body feels relaxed and often heavy (Weitsenhoffer, 1989).

Hypnosis is a very efficient and powerful technique; it is not a quick fix or cure. Some people look for a magical quick fix to stop smoking or rapidly lose weight. These people often don't want to put any effort into achieving these changes. They want the magical change without any effort. You need to be willing to make changes for optimal results to be experienced. Hypnosis has also been used for entertainment purposes in auditoriums around the world filled with audiences in awe and disbelief. This often gives people an idea of mind control and unethical use of power and creates fear. In the context of this book, hypnosis is used as a therapeutic tool to effect beneficial changes within the subconscious mind. The aim is to reduce symptoms that are limiting a person's ability to live a healthy life.

Hypnosis as a therapeutic technique can vary in many forms. It can be used as a way of teaching someone to relax or release a phobia. Relaxation is quite important when doing deep work, as it sends a signal to the brain that you are safe. When you are relaxed, you increase your brain's ability to absorb information. In a relaxed state, you are more suggestible, that means you increase your ability to take on suggestions given to you. This accelerates healing and the implementation of desired changes.

Hypnosis works directly with the deepest programming of the subconscious mind. In the subconscious, you store your beliefs, memories, thought and emotional patterns. Your subconscious houses the programs that drive your daily functioning. When you work with the subconscious mind, you can directly work with these programs. You can release the limitations you have developed over the years or as a result of a direct situation. This leads the way to helping you overcome limiting beliefs, emotions, and behaviors that trouble you. I conduct a process I call emotional cleansing. You begin to eliminate all the negativity that is holding you back. Once you have cleansed and made room, you can now create. Cleansing out all the toxic patterns allows you to have the freedom to think more clearly.

Clearing out the negative patterns gives you the ability to step out of survival mode. When you are calmer, you can create clearly. You can boost your self-esteem, improve your self-talk, and feel more love. You can create hypnotic suggestions that will reinforce the changes. For example, I often tell my patients to imagine that every time they drink water, they will feel calm. This is powerful, it uses an everyday activity to reinforce your work. Slowly, you can start to weave in little aspects that reinforce changes made in your subconscious mind. These suggestions are embedded deep in your subconscious mind. The subconscious mind uses your imagination and suggestibility. It can combine an image with direct suggestion. For example, I may say, "Imagine you are walking down a pathway; each step allows you to feel more relaxed." I'm getting you to imagine the pathway. Then I'm giving you the suggestion to feel more relaxed with every step you take. The body is relaxed and the mind is aware; this creates the perfect environment for change.

When you are in hypnosis, your perception is altered. You have greater sensory perception, experiencing sensations that go beyond your ordinary conscious states. For example, you may feel your body so relaxed it almost feels asleep yet you are fully aware of the hypnotist's words. You are aware but in a dreamy kind of state. You may feel completely immersed in a narrative and actually "feel" like you are physically there. If I guide a patient to imagine they are putting their feet in a stream of water, they may feel the water. I suggest they feel the warm sun on their skin, they actually feel the warmth. The mind is able to differentiate between different temperatures of warm sun and cold water while being aware of my voice. It's almost as if you tap into the ability to be in multiple spaces simultaneously.

The experience of hypnosis is a very personal one; everyone responds differently and improves at a different pace. In that state of altered consciousness, relaxation creates the perfect environment for change. The door to the subconscious mind mysteriously opens. You now have access to the programs embedded deep within the subconscious mind. When you gain access to this beautiful part of the mind, you can begin to create lasting change. You begin to release all these negative patterns that have formed throughout time, and you can create new ones. By doing this, you begin to create patterns that are more positive, more empowering, and especially designed by you for you! It does sound magical, though, right? It can be in its own right, just not in the quick fix kind of way some people seek out. The magic is much greater than you could ever imagine. The unseen mysterious change unfolding is magical. When you step into the courage to dive deep into the subconscious, possibilities are endless. I have successfully applied the use of hypnotherapy to hundreds of patients for a wide variety of issues. I've experienced people letting go of decades of grief, resentment, and anger. I've seen pain disappear and health return to optimal states of well-being. Hypnosis is a very effective and pleasant way of dealing with so many burdens.

It is my opinion that hypnosis can therapeutically improve almost all ailments. This is a big statement, so let me elaborate on what I mean by this. If you have a chronic illness such as irritable bowel syndrome or heart disease, hypnosis may not "cure" the disease, but it can do something profound. Hypnosis can significantly lower the level of stress and negative emotions such as worry and fear associated with the disease. By doing this, you reduce the chemical secretions creating stress and improve body functioning. All illnesses have emotions connected to them (Rossi, 2007). Ultimately, everything starts and stops in the mind. By getting on top of your emotions and mindset, you get on top of your physical health also. An active relationship unfolds between your mind and your physical well-being.

External circumstances like a car accident can affect your health. Whether you suffer as a result of that car accident is greatly dependant on your mindset. It also depends on how you relate to your body, your self-talk, your stress levels. Hypnosis can train the mind, strengthen the body, and heal beyond imagination. Hypnosis can also be used to go into regressions to heal parts of your past. There have been many cases documented of people that have healed psychological and physical symptoms through hypnotic regressions (Weiss, 1998). The power of the mind is possibly the most underestimated. Scientific research has shown how powerful placebo effects can be. Studies have demonstrated that people treated with a placebo pill for depression not only relieved symptoms but brain scans showed changes in the prefrontal cortex (Leuchter et al., 2002). This goes to show how powerful your mind is. If you think you are getting a treatment and it changes your brain imagine all the other changes unfolding daily. This is where hypnosis is wonderful; you literally use your mind's power to change the thoughts and feelings you have to create real changes in your body.

Hypnosis has shown me what the power of imagination can create. The combination of perfectly crafted words and scenarios can soothe the brain, motivate the psyche, and allow your heart to expand. It has the power to create empowered action and positively influence your life. I humbly owe much of my transformation in creating a beautiful mind to hypnosis.

Exercise:

- Write down your limiting thoughts and beliefs.
- What areas in your life are causing stress?
- What situations create fear, insecurities, worry, or sadness.
- What sensations in your body do you have when you notice these negative aspects?
  - e.g., I worry I'm going to be judged at work all the time. I have stomach aches every morning on my way to work
  - e.g., I'm afraid my partner will leave me. I go through scenarios in my head of what they will tell me I did wrong. I feel pain and tension in my jaw.
  - e.g., I'm not good enough at my job and fear they will figure it out and fire me. I feel nervous all the time. I have tension headaches.
- Now I want you to take a deep breath.
- Focus on a spot on the wall in front of you.
- Have the intention of releasing all the negative emotions and programs you carry with you.
- Take a deep breath and, on the exhale, close your eyes.
- Focus on the top of your head and fill your body with a nice golden light from head to toe.
- Feel this light relaxing your muscles and your mind.
- Now imagine you are in front of a fire; notice the flames, the colors, and the warmth.
- Imagine writing down all the negative programs you have within you on a piece of paper.
- Visualize scrunching up that piece of paper and throwing it into the fire.

- Watch it burn, and be released permanently out of your mind, out of your body, out of your life.
- Take a deep breath and feel the sense of relaxation expanding through your body, a sense of relief.
- Imagine having a glass of water and letting the water cleanse you and revitalize you.
- Feel your mind is clear and ready to have empowering, confident, healthy, and loving programs installed.
- Take a deep breath, and, as your body expands with air, your cells fill with confidence, health, and love. Do this three times and feel your cells being programmed.
- Say to yourself: "I am empowered, I am confident, I am healthy, I am loved" three times.
- To finish this exercise, grab a piece of paper and write this down:
  - I am empowered, I am confident, I am healthy, I am loved
  - I feel empowered, I feel confident, I feel healthy, I feel loved
  - It is safe to feel empowered, confident, healthy, and loved
- Get into the habit of doing this regularly (daily if you can). Give your brain the right instructions.
- Begin to create positive feelings and circumstances in your life.

I AM EMPOWERED

I AM CONFIDENT

I AM HEALTHY

I AM LOVED

I AM SAFE

I AM CALM

I AM INSPIRED

I AM BEAUTIFUL

I AM AMAZING

We are walking fields of memories,

Created from the beginning of time.

Keep walking and consciously creating.

Kalí

CHAPTER 3

STRESS & HEALING

Spontaneous Healing Unfolds, Chile 2010

I was sitting in a cold and clinical medical room; my palms were sweaty, my heart racing. I was being told I needed to have yet another operation. I had struggled with endometriosis and polycystic ovarian syndrome (PCOS) for years. In my early twenties, I'd had several procedures already. The last operation didn't fix it, why should I believe this one would? I'd lost faith in the medical model. I'd been rushed too many times to the emergency room only to be sent home again, drugged up with morphine and dreading the next episode. The pain was excruciating. Against medical recommendations, I declined their offer to operate on me again. I decided it was time to go into the deepest core of my subconscious and begin to explore the root cause of the issue. This was beginning to happen more regularly and it was limiting me in more ways than I liked. After deciding against surgery, I put myself in the hands of hypnotherapist, Barbara. I sensed there was something deeper going on that conventional medicine couldn't change. I was determined to heal, to let go of whatever I wasn't aware of that was holding onto me. I went to hypnotherapy with the aim of reducing the symptoms I was experiencing. I lay on the hypnotherapist's couch, willing to dive into my subconscious. What was about to unfold was much deeper than what I expected. Barbara took me into a gentle trance, but, suddenly, I found myself somewhere else. She told me to go back to the root cause of my issue. I slipped into a completely different time and space. I was going into a spontaneous hypnotic regression. I had visions of places I seemed to recognize, but had never been to in this life. I felt sensations in my body and visualized events unfolding in my mind's eye. These were separate from my actual experience at that time and space. Barbara inquired what was happening; a dialogue opened up. I was lying on a bed surrounded by women wearing white dresses. I was in an old cold stone building, heavily pregnant, getting ready to give birth (this was happening in my regression). I had an awareness that I was in the hypnotherapist's office, but I was also aware of an alternate reality in this event I was reliving. I could see myself lying on the bed with several women around me. I felt warm and wet; I couldn't decipher if it was my actual body or my body in the event I was recalling. I could see myself as if I were watching a movie and experiencing it at the same time. There was an overlap in consciousness. All I could say to Barbara was that I felt wet and warm and started to think that maybe I'd wet myself.

I lost track of time and seemed to lose perception. Then it felt like I slipped away into what felt like a deep sleep; it felt relieving, restful, and peaceful. It felt like the moment you notice you are falling asleep, for a split second you are aware you're drifting off.

I had actually experienced dying in this past life. I died giving birth. The baby had also died. The death felt peaceful, but I could feel grief that I processed in hypnosis and also later on. During my processing, I felt as if I had made peace with that lifetime. I made peace with my body; I made peace with death. I came out of that experience feeling sad, relieved, warm, and surprisingly relaxed. I didn't go there expecting that! It just happened. People sometimes go into spontaneous regressions. I'd learned to allow these experiences to just unfold and not analyze them too much. Maybe there was something in my subconscious that needed healing. It felt like I had made peace with something in my past that had subconsciously haunted me without even knowing. I walked away feeling calm, bewildered, and in slight disbelief. When I arrived home, I had the longest nap in history. I didn't give it much thought, detached from the outcome, and carried on with my life. The days passed by and I would journal my visions or insights about this experience.

Several months later, I returned to the surgeon's office for a check-up. There were no sign of cysts in my ovaries. There was no pain, symptoms, or indicators that my body had PCOS or endometriosis at all. The surgeon was baffled, but told me to go back in another six months just in case. I walked away delighted, as if I were holding onto a secret bit of magic. That was the last of the medical issues I had with that story of my body and that was over ten years ago.

Healing old wounds sometimes goes beyond the physical body. Traditional Western medicine can do wonders, but it doesn't always heal. I've learned that healing encompasses all aspects of the human existence. Sometimes, it lies in your cellular memory, your energetic field, or spiritual realm. Sometimes, it may even lie in aspects of us we are totally unaware of. Healing is also often reported in near-death experiences. People who have had near-death experiences (NDE) and have been ill with cancer, for example, have healed as a result of their NDE. They reconciled with aspects of their lives that held them hostage in sick bodies. Many people who have had NDEs have come back to healed bodies. They returned to minds willing to let go of the past and bodies filled with life force (Moorjani, 2012). They made a decision to come back to live in pure vitality and unconditional love. If you look hard enough, you will find evidence of medical miracles like this all over the world. This is the power of the mind-body connection.

Stressed Out!

Stress is today's number one killer. In 2018, the Australian Bureau of Statistics reported that suicide is the leading cause of death for people aged 15-44. I don't know about you, but I find that extremely disturbing. There are similar statistics around the globe of stress leading to suicide. Modern societies have created such intense pressure on people that it is literally killing humans globally. Stress is related to most of the leading causes of death around the globe. It has been linked to cancer, heart disease, respiratory illnesses, and mental illness.

You see, when your body is under prolonged stress, it begins to strain your immune function, CNS, and brain chemistry (Segerstrom et al., 2004). Prolonged or chronic stress is often the result of life's daily stressors: traffic, work pressures, financial stress, relationship difficulties, and social pressures. Sometimes, life events can cause significantly high levels of stress that will create a more profound impact. Some of these events are life changing like job loss, migration, illness, death of a loved one, and accidents. However, the way you approach these life experiences will determine how significantly it will affect you. Your perception of your ability to cope will determine the impact stress has on you. Stress also affects your cognitive capacities, making you unable to concentrate and think clearly. When you are stressed, you are more irritable and more likely to lash out at others or withdraw (Fisch et al., 2017). Stress not only creates physical and emotional imbalances but also disrupts your ability to cope with life. It impacts your relationships and causes disharmony in your social world.

How you deal with stress is crucial to your well-being. Stress is part of life; learning how to deal with it in positive ways is valuable. Hypnotherapy and mindfulness techniques have been scientifically proven to be effective techniques in stress management (Fisch et al., 2017). It is so important to build emotional resilience early in life and teach young people to cope well. Studies show that childhood stress affects your immune system. Longitudinal studies have found that people who experienced lots of stress in their childhood had higher rates of physical illness in their adult years compared to others who hadn't experienced stressful events. It can have prolonged effects that really diminishes a person's quality of life (Danese et al., 2017). This is why you often see children who are going through major life disruptions experiencing a variety of physical symptoms. Oftentimes, children don't have the language to express their feelings or experiences, but this emotional energy expresses itself through the body in physical symptoms and behavioral issues. The old wounds you carry, if untreated, can wreak havoc in your adult body.

During my time working as a health psychologist at The Wesley Hospital, I was privileged to observe this very concept in the making. I was working in a pain management program. I assessed patients upon intake, ran psychoeducation sessions, individual consultations, and discharge assessments. I observed patients from the moment they walked in the door until they left at the end of the day. The program was comprehensive, it included exercise physiology, physiotherapy, occupational therapy, nutrition, hydrotherapy, psychoeducation, and medical assessment.

I could observe them in different scenarios. I noticed the patients who were angry, resentful, frustrated, and sad would take a longer time to recover. They were less friendly and focused on their pain in every conversation. They reported higher levels of pain and did not feel in control of their situation. They ruminated, blamed, and resisted suggestions given to them. They were more defiant, argumentative, and simply did not accept their condition. The patients who had similar clinical symptoms but had a positive outlook had clinically significant improvements. These patients were open and willing to learn new ways of engaging with their bodies. They found a way to accept the injury and forgive the incident. They established relationships with others more easily and provided support among the group. These were the patients who recovered the quickest and had decreased pain levels and increased mobility. They had a greater sense of control and were more hopeful and happier about their futures. Follow ups showed that those patients with a more positive demeanor continued to improve over time. Most of them returning to their lives fully functioning and integrated. Whereas the patients who had a lot of emotional turmoil and were not open to change didn't continue to improve. They had an increase in pain levels and did not integrate back into their lives successfully. The attitude with which you face life's hurdles will determine your health and your quality of life.

As a health psychologist, I'm interested in showing you how your body and mind work. Let's have a look at how you can begin to assess areas of your life so you can become your own chemical engineer. I want you to think about all the things your body needs.

It needs oxygen, food, water, sleep, exercise, and shelter. We are social creatures, so we also need a good dose of social interaction. So, first things first, if you're not giving your body what it needs to function it simply won't function at its best. It's unrealistic to think that you should be healthy if you don't get enough sleep. If you exercise a lot but don't eat well, your body won't be happy. If you work overtime and rush around stressed, your body won't be happy. It's about balance and quality. The quality of sleep, food, and people all impact your well-being. Are you feeding your body nourishing foods? Are you socializing with the right people? Are you getting quality sleep? Is your life balanced? These are aspects of your life I want you to think about. Just like the quality of your life depends on the quality of the questions you ask, so does the quality of everything else. After you have met your basic needs, think about healing your wounds and moving up toward higher levels of functioning, eventually reaching optimum well-being and self-actualization.

Maslow's model of human needs provides a good understanding of basic requirements. Abraham Maslow was an American-born psychologist. He developed what is commonly known as Maslow's Hierarchy of Needs. Maslow described that all stages needed to be fulfilled prior to the next stage being achieved. For example, basic needs (i.e., physiological needs: water, food, and shelter) need to be fulfilled before moving up to the next level. Safety needs come before psychological needs. Then psychological needs: sense of belonging, love, relationships, need to be fulfilled before moving up. Lastly is self-transcendence, creating a life of purpose and meaning after realizing your fullest potential and reaching your goals.

Maslow's Hierarchy of Needs

If you think about it, it actually makes a lot of sense. How can you feel safe when you are starving and don't have shelter? How can you feel a sense of belonging if you're unhealthy and unable to participate in society? Understanding some of these concepts is important for your own development. It also helps you to understand other people's situations more compassionately. You will most likely come across people who are less fortunate than you; it is important to understand they may not have the basic needs necessary to be friendly or connected. People under a lot of stress are often angry, irritable, and on edge. Next time you are faced with this, take a moment to remember they may be struggling with lack of food, lack of safety, or health issues. I want you to take a moment and think about the complexity of human existence. Think about your life and your needs. How do you feel you are meeting your own needs? Are you just surviving or thriving? Most people dream about reaching their goals and realizing their fullest potential. Very few actually take the time to explore how to get there. Once you get there, you have the luxury of exploring your purpose and meaning in your life. I'm going to take you through a journey discovering how to best meet your needs. The purpose here is to illustrate daily things you can do to boost your well-being.

Importance of Sleep

You will most like notice that if you don't sleep well, you're off kilter. You might feel a bit grumpy and irritable after a poor night's sleep. You rush off, you're not thinking straight, and you start the day discombobulated. Society has glorified busyness and technology; this is massively disrupting sleep around the globe. People are living in societies that are fast-paced, overstimulated, and chaotic. This creates a lot of stress on your body. By the time you're getting ready for bed, you're mostly tired but also wired. Over time, disrupted sleep patterns will begin to take their toll and start to affect every aspect of your life. Sleep issues are strongly related to depression and mood disorders (Srinivasan et al., 2006). You simply don't function well with poor sleep; it's one of the most important factors that will impact your mood and well-being.

Sleep is largely governed by melatonin, a hormone secreted by your pineal gland. It has an important role in regulating your sleep cycles. Melatonin is light sensitive, so it is naturally secreted at night time. Melatonin also affects your mood and immunity. I want you to think about your sleep hygiene, essentially your bedtime routine. How much exposure to artificial light are you having in the evening? Excessive exposure to lights in your home and on your phone, television, and computers slows down the secretion of melatonin. It's essentially giving the brain the signal to "stay awake." So, when you go to bed with your phone or the TV the last thing you see and you don't fall asleep easily, you know why. I often hear from patients saying they have racings thoughts as soon as they go to bed. Think about why this might be. You're running around all day, stressed, overstretched, time poor, overstimulated. You stop and go to bed. You haven't allowed your body to slow down. You haven't calmed your CNS from the day's stress. Suddenly, all the things you've done and the things you need to do call for your attention.

You've overstretched your body with activity and flooded it with stress hormones all day. And now you're putting on the brakes. It's like giving a child a bag of candy and saying, "Now go sit quietly and relax." Impossible. Your sleep is essential to your well-being. Sleep affects your mood, energy, immunity, and focus to name a few. It deserves your attention and respect. Getting the right amount of sleep is important, figure out what is ideal for you. Create a routine that allows you to stick to regular bedtime and waking cycles.

Create a good sleep routine:

- Dim the lights in your home at night time.
- Turn the noise down: music, conversations, television.
- Put calming music on.
- Have a bath or a hot shower to relax your body.
- Put away your electronic devices at least an hour before sleep.
- Allow yourself some time to reflect, feel gratitude, and close the day.
- Meditate, pray, or listen to a guided meditation.
- Journal and make a to-do list for the next so you dump your thoughts onto paper.

There is also something magical about the time window around sleep. Your subconscious mind is most receptive upon the moment of waking and just before sleep. Whatever you listen to or focus on at bedtime will expand. Be mindful of what you're feeding your mind. Listening to guided meditations or binaural sounds at this time can be soothing for the brain and empowering for your mind.

Increase Daily Practices That Empower You

Shake It Up!

Humans were made to move, to use muscles and be physically active. Physical activity is part of your natural state, it is necessary for well-being. The benefits of physical activity are endless, it creates powerful changes in your body and in your mind. It has been scientifically proven that exercise improves mood in people experiencing depression (Lane et al., 2001). Exercise also helps to reduce the symptoms associated with anxiety (Attila, 2003). Your body was made to be used in beautiful ways. You see, it is all energy. When you feel anxious, you have too much nervous energy running through your body. When you go for a walk, exercise begins to release stress hormones like cortisol and, after a little while, you begin to feel much better. When you are sitting down, holding onto all that nervous energy, it has nowhere to go. Walk it off, shake it out, run it out of your system. It doesn't take much; take control of your body and use it well.

Research suggests that 10 minutes of exercises can lower anxiety and improve mood (Hansen et al., 2001). It doesn't take long to look after yourself when you realize how important exercise is. You simply need to make it a priority. You weren't made to live sedentary lives in front of screens under artificial lighting. It might be part of the "norm" nowadays, but that doesn't mean it's healthy.

Exercise allows your body to release stress built up throughout the day. It allows you to pump oxygen and blood through your body, nourishing you. It strengthens your muscles and clears your mind. You were made to move; it is in your DNA. Movement allows you to use your senses, tune in to your body. You're looking after this beautiful machine, your body, that carries you around. The more you look after it the better it will run. When you feel good in your own skin, you feel better about yourself. I want you to think of everything you do as either boosting your well-being or damaging it. Exercise first thing in the morning, this energizes and activates your metabolic system. Energy keeps running and moving through your body for hours. This increases endorphins that allow you to feel good, more powerful, more alert. When you're exercising, listen to something inspirational that motivates you. You will begin to associate exercising with feeling motivated. By doing this you're creating neural pathways in your brain of feeling good and exercising. You will feel more pumped, motivated, and happy about your choices. Motivation will increase your chances of continuing to do it. Physical exercise also helps you sleep better. If you sleep better, you feel better.

If you combine physical exercise with nature, it's even more powerful. Being in nature can improve your sense of calm, connectedness, and mood (Li, 2018). Exercising in nature can have rejuvenating effects, it makes you feel more alive and clear-headed. Use your body wisely, look after it while you have it, and take great care of it. It is your faithful servant; love it! Exercise is good not only for your body but also for your soul. Do good things for your soul!

Put Your Arms Up

The way you hold yourself communicates to the world how you are feeling. When you are feeling low, you most likely walk with your head held down. When you are happy, you're walking with a spring in your step, strong, open, and poised. Posture plays an important role in your relationship with emotions. If you observe nature, there are examples everywhere of this. A cat that is afraid looks very different to one that is relaxed basking in the sun. Darwin observed that humans display particular bodily movements as emotional expression. He describes people holding their head down with droopy eyes when experiencing grief. When describing joy, Darwin states "from the excitement of pleasure, the circulation becomes more rapid...the brain being stimulated by the increase flow of blood reacts on the mental powers; lively ideas pass still more rapidly through the mind, and affections are warmed" (Darwin, 1872). I think it's beautiful how Darwin describes this, excitement of pleasure, lively ideas, affections are warmed; it's like remembering a beautiful childhood moment.

Postures and expressions are the body's way of communicating to the world. How you hold yourself has great power; it has the power to affect how you feel and how you portray yourself. When you are in an open posture, you feel more open to the world. It's important to start noticing how you hold yourself. There is a constant relationship unfolding between postures and emotions and vice versa. Postures can play an important role in activating emotions with specific poses. Part of having an empowered mind is knowing how to use your body to activate the changes you want. If you want to feel confident, stand up straight, hold your head high, your shoulders relaxed and wide. Your brain creates associations all the time. It will associate a posture of droopy head, slouched shoulders, and lowered gaze to feelings of low mood. Similarly, it has an association of joy and achievement when you stand strong with your arms up high making a V. Consciously use your body to create change.

Sometimes in therapy I might get my patients to change their bodily positions. If a patient is describing a stressful situation sitting on the couch, I'll suggest they sit or lie on the floor. Occasionally I'll get a strange look from them, but most will gladly follow my suggestion. Then while they're sitting or lying on the floor, I'll ask them to recount the same scenario. Oftentimes, they don't seem to be able to access the severity of emotion they were experiencing in the sitting position. This is interesting. You see, as adults you spend most of your time sitting on chairs. Rarely do adults go on the ground. When you do, it's to play with children, sit down and relax, at the beach etc. Your mind has created and association to feeling relaxed when on the ground. So, you might find that changing your physical position might change how you feel. There is also something very primal about sitting on the ground that makes you feel grounded.

Just Breathe

You enter this world with your first breath; it is life force. You exit your life with your last breath. Breathing is life, it deserves your attention. It's well known that stress creates shallow breathing, you feel tight in your chest and you might experience shortness of breath. These are some of the symptoms of stress, changes in your breathing. I'm sure you can relate being given a paper bag to breathe into if you're panicking. These techniques encourage deep breathing; it's a quick and effective way to slow you down. Deep breathing relaxes your nervous system, almost immediately. The effects of deep breathing are countless. It clears your mind, calms your nerves and brings you back to the present. Allowing you to connect to your body mindfully. Ancient yogis believed that by controlling your breathing, you control your mind (McCall, 2007). Breathwork has been used in many healing modalities, and it has great power to transform your body. It is one of the most accessible self-healing techniques you can apply.

Getting into a habit of deep breathing or mindful breathing allows you to slow down. Wherever you are, you can always stop and take a deep breath. When you slow down, you're essentially getting out of survival mode. It is the quickest way you can communicate to the body you are "safe." Remember Maslow's hierarchy of needs, you must feel safe to keep evolving. In order to achieve an empowered mindset, you must first feel calm and safe in your body. When you feel safe, you can work on achieving higher states of consciousness. So, take a deep breath and get started. There are many great breathing techniques that are used for healing and transformation; they go beyond the scope of this book. I encourage you to start with daily practice of noticing your breathing and incorporating deep breathing in your daily routines.

Who's Coming?

In addition to good sleep, exercising, postures, and breathing, there are social aspects to take into consideration: the company you keep. As humans, we love to socialize, some more than others, but social aspects of life shape us. Socializing begins from a very early stage in life; social structures create opportunities for experiences to unfold. You might be a bit of an introvert or more of a social butterfly; it doesn't matter. Socializing is still part of the human condition. It is a part of life that allows you to express who you are among others. The people you surround yourself with can greatly influence how you function. Although I want you to create a strong internal environment and be self-approving, you will inevitably engage with others. Who you surround yourself with and the experiences you have together will create emotional bonds. If your friends are negative, every time you are with them, you are bonding to them and to the negativity. Be mindful of what you are bonding to. I encourage you to surround yourself with magnificent people. Read about inspiring people. Make a habit of following positive role models in your family, your friends, and society. Remember that your brain is constantly making meaning of the world around you.

When you begin to surround yourself with wonderful people, you get inspired. You feel motivated, you mirror magnificence, you feed off each other; so, bring your best self to the party. Think about interactions you might have had that leave you feeling great. Choose those ones more frequently than the other ones. Start being more selective of how you spend your time; create spaces in your life that bond you to magnificence. This happens in exactly the same way that people complain and whine about how bad life is. When you do this with others, it gives you a sense you're on the same team. Your opinions are validated by one another. You find allies who understand you and reinforce your beliefs. The danger in having company that is negative is that you're creating bonds with the other person through victimhood. Then you become attached to doing this with your friends, your colleagues, your family. The trouble here is that you're literally creating neural pathways that bond you to that person through negativity. Your relationship is now founded on whining.

Have you ever noticed that, sometimes, parts of you come out only with certain people? Maybe you're a generally happy person. But when you get together with your friends Annie or Frank, you turn into someone else. The whiney negative part of you shows up to the party. You will most likely feel agitated walking away from that catch up. On the flip side, if you have bubbly friends, you're likely to feel energized and happy as you leave those friends. You are mirroring and affecting each other's energy fields all the time. Notice how you feel after you walk away from people. Once again, be self-aware and begin to observe your life with curiosity.

I'm sure you've had the experience of meeting someone charismatic and uplifting. Generally, you end up feeling invigorated and full of vitality. It lightens up your life. It lifts the heaviness of the responsibilities you carry. This is the experience you want to foster within your brain. You can become that person in your own unique way. Strive to be the one who leaves a situation better than when you arrived just by being yourself, the best version of yourself, the one you're consciously creating right here right now. I hope you can see that we're all interconnected. Everyone is giving and receiving constantly, strengthening and weakening patterns. Strengthen the patterns that nourish you and weaken the ones that damage you. I encourage you to take full responsibility for the company you keep. Take mindful responsibility for the conversations you have. Make every spare moment an opportunity to fill your mind with joy. Talk about joy, be joy, inspire joy in others.

What Did You Just Say?

As you have noticed by now, communication is incredibly important. The way you communicate with yourself, first, is the most important of all. The way you speak to yourself, the way you reprimand yourself, and encourage yourself will determine how you approach people and how you build relationships. This will also impact the type of environment you begin to design for yourself. No other species has such a developed and complex system elaborated to communicate with its intonations, cultural norms, societal norms, class structures, and political correctness. People have constructed such elaborate and complex models of engaging with one another that it often gets lost in translation. It is often misused. It is regularly misunderstood. Unfortunately, it is also commonly abused. Yet it shapes your human experience.

As previously mentioned in Chapter 2 with Katie's story, you can see how words can be used to truly harm another. They can also be a source of love and inspiration, especially when you speak from your heart.

Thank You!

Expressing your gratitude toward a person can be a powerful experience. Gratitude plays a significant role in positive reinforcement in relationships. Gratitude allows you to feel love. When this love is expressed, you create a change within the other. From the most basic mammals to the most complex humans, positive reinforcement shapes behaviors. When you begin the journey of self-discovery, you become aware of who you are. You start to notice who you are, what you like, what helps or serves you. By understanding this, you can become aware of how your own behavior can begin to shape experiences. You can influence the behaviors of those around you. Gratitude is a powerful way that positively reinforces behaviors of those around you. It makes you feel grateful; it acknowledges another and shapes behaviors. Sounds pretty good to me. By harnessing this awareness, you can shape and craft the world you live in.

In psychology, the term "operant conditioning" explores this. Operant conditioning was established by Burrhus Frederic

Skinner, an American psychologist. Skinner examined the reward and punishment model to understand behavior and conditioning. Skinner noted that people are more likely to repeat a behavior if it has a pleasant association. He also found that people are likely to avoid a situation that causes pain or has grave consequences. If a behavior that causes pleasure is reinforced, it is likely to occur again. Reinforcement strengthens the behavior. Think about how you scold children or give them medals. It helps them shape an understanding of what is acceptable and desirable. You are training their brain to learn through conditioning. Adults are much the same, you learn what others love by the reactions they have when you do something for them.

What kind of reinforcements are you applying in your own life? You are constantly sending messages to the world, your loved ones, yourself. You're playing an active role in reinforcing or weakening behaviors. For example, if I notice a family member has done something nice like wash the dishes, but I don't say anything, that act goes unnoticed. The likelihood of it occurring again may be slim because the person may not feel valued or acknowledged and may not do it again. If I complain every time they leave a mess, I'm only focusing on the negative aspect of their behaviors. They may retaliate by saying, "What's the point; you never notice when I do something right anyway." Can you relate to this? What, if I come home, notice the dishes got done, and express my gratitude? I'm reinforcing that behavior. I might thank them and give them a hug. I'm expressing my feelings and following it through with a loving action, the hug. I have married the words of appreciation with the act of a kind hug. The hug secretes hormones of oxytocin that allows me to bond with that person. This begins to shape the behavior of the other person. It's like your boss telling you that you did a great job. It makes you want to do it again; most people love being acknowledged. The more you can recognize good acts, the more likely they are to occur. It's a great habit to get into. Most people are always focusing on the negative. Switch it around!

I understand not every good act needs to be followed by a hug. You may not be a hugger, but allow yourself to at least notice and acknowledge the kind acts others do for you. When you acknowledge the positive acts others do, you step into gratitude. Gratitude activates a sense of love, it's a healing experience for all parties involved. This secretes chemicals that make you feel good. When you do this repeatedly, you begin to establish a pattern. The brain learns that this feels good, so it will repeat it. It focuses attention and looks for these actions; it will try to recreate the experience. Your brain will want to access that state of reward and pleasure more regularly. Wanting more of that feel-good chemical cocktail you just gave it.

The more you appreciate and acknowledge everyday acts in others, the more likely they are to occur. You can shape the world around you by positively reinforcing behaviors you desire. This is also applicable with how you speak to yourself. Be awesome enough to tell yourself when you've done a great job. You'll build a strong internal sense of self-approval.

Reinforcing behaviors can be a tricky thing to navigate in relationships. Imagine you come home from work and your partner has had a rough day. They lash out and yell at you. You can engage and give them attention and fuel the fire. Or you can decide to go out for a walk. You gently say, "I'm just going to let you be for a few minutes while I go for a walk." You don't ignore them; you just get out of the way. You might even ask if they'd like to go for a walk with you. You don't engage in it by fueling it with a reaction, discussion, and possibly a fight. The art of not taking things personally is really valuable here. When you are able to rise above your emotions, rise above your ego, you are empowered. You can choose what to step into and get involved in and what to softly step away from. When you respectfully step away from situations that may be inflammatory, you are saying, "I'm not playing; I'm not engaging." People want to engage and get a reaction. By stepping away from it, you weaken their behavior of lashing out toward you. Maybe they had the experience as children that their mother only engaged when they were kicking and screaming. Maybe this is what they learned. It's no one's fault; it just is. They learned that if there wasn't any confrontational attention, they weren't important. They weren't seen; they weren't loved. The more you can apply your understanding of how people function, the smoother your relationships will be. Go back to thinking about Maslow's hierarchy of needs. If your partner is tired or had a bad day at work, they might not have the capacity to be nice at that time. It doesn't make it right or wrong; it just is. If you can see this, you have a choice as to how you engage. It is up to you to pick your battles, choose where your energy goes, and how you engage. Letting some things slide and pulling away from being judgmental can be a real gift.

Having open conversations with your loved ones is crucial in the development of healthy relationships. Being able to discuss things when they're not happening right there and then is a valuable skill to learn. Say to your partner that you understand some days they're grumpy and you feel it's best to give them some time out. Explain that when you walk away (lovingly), you do so to allow them to cool off so you don't end up in a fight. These discussions allow you to have clear communication about your feelings and the intention behind your actions. There is no room for misinterpretation, no room for taking things personally. This might be delicate to navigate at first but very worthwhile in the long term. At the end of the day, make time for gratitude. Make time to express your gratitude and love for the people you have chosen to have in your life. Gratitude fills you with a sense of love; it softens the hard edges of life. If you can start and finish your days with gratitude, that will be what your subconscious mind focuses on.

Daily Acts of Empowerment

- Commit to implementing changes today right now! Don't leave it until Monday or tomorrow; use your momentum to start right now.
- Become the very best in your field. Become so good that you become irreplaceable. It doesn't need to be something big; it could be a simple thing. Become such a valuable asset that you stand out through your greatness.
- When you commit to doing something, help yourself; avoid distractions. Turn your phone off; focus on what you're doing.
- Do what's hardest first and then reward yourself by doing something more enjoyable. Be smart in how you use your energy; use it for the most challenging aspects first.
- Allow yourself some time to think daily. People are so busy all day long, the only time they really stop is when they hit the bed. This is not the ideal time to think, this is when you need to unwind and drift off to sleep.
- Allocate yourself a time to stop and meditate a little. Have novel ideas, this fosters a healthy brain. Contemplate life's wonders, ideas, dreams.
- At the end of your day, ask yourself some questions:
  - What could you have done differently?
  - What things did you waste time on that you recognize you don't want to keep wasting time on?

○ Are you spending too much time on your phone and social media?

- Ask yourself what are the three things you did well today?
- What made you feel good?
- What are the three things you'd like to celebrate, that you feel grateful for? Did you go for a longer walk today? Did you handle an argument lovingly? Did you express gratitude to someone you care about? Did you listen to an inspiring podcast on your way to work instead of getting frustrated by traffic?

When you do this, you can take account of your day's events. You become aware of what's going on, where you're not doing so great, and the areas you'd like to improve. By doing this, you're actually being fair with your assessment of your day and your life. Celebrating small daily wins allows you to foster a sense of satisfaction and confidence in yourself. You allow yourself to feel good about who you are. It doesn't matter how small the win is; acknowledge it. Improve a few things you consider important in your everyday life, making small incremental changes. Every day, you'll get stronger, fitter, and clearer in your efforts. This increases your self-confidence and well-being. Welcome new opportunities into your life. By doing that, you're watering the seeds you've planted; if you do this every day, it will start to grow just like a little plant. Whatever you focus on, you fuel.

Einstein's definition of insanity is "doing the same thing and expecting a different result"

You Can Do Better

Become your best friend. Become the person who inspires you the most, the person who laughs at life's silly occurrences. Be the person who makes someone else's day. Build your internal empire by becoming your very best self. By observing how you think, feel, and behave, you'll start to figure out who you are more clearly. Approach this as a renovation project. You have a strong foundation already; otherwise, you wouldn't be reading this book. There is always something to improve or do a little differently, so start becoming the version of yourself that makes you proud of who you are. Make small daily changes to who you are, always moving forwards. Allow yourself to shine brightly on the inside; start with positive self-talk and great self-care. The more you do this, the more you'll feel love and compassion for yourself and others. As you build a strong internal state, you will emanate this energy. Life will start loving you back, bringing you all those things that are vibrating at that same frequency as you. You'll start feeling more magnetic; you'll start attracting more positive people. You might even notice you start to smile more; generally, people will smile back at you. Allow your change to start from within.

People often look toward the outside and wait for the right circumstances to make a change. Real change occurs from the inside out. The more magnificent your internal world the better your life will be. Start applying all the things you've learned so far to improve your life. Look after your body with great care and respect, rest it, move it, and feed it well. Apply positive coping mechanisms to reduce stress: daily breathing exercises, meditation, journaling. All of these things put together will make you feel better on multiple levels. You'll strengthen your biology, your mind, and your outer world. You'll start feeling more self-love, more confidence. It will naturally glow from within you. You'll start feeling happier, more abundant, more worthy. When this happens, you want to share your joy with others. You begin to realize that it lies within you. It's exciting when you feel this way, you can't help but sharing with everyone you love. And if you've constructed the right social circles, you'll want to share it with them. Share your joy with all those people who want the best for you, the ones who support and encourage you. This sharing gets contagious; people will want to know what is making you feel so good. You see, when you start to shine you give others permission to shine too, you begin to transform into that person everyone wants to be around because you're glowing. This starts to feel magical, and it changes your life.

When you start to feel like this, you'll realize what you've created is unlimited. You've tapped into an unlimited source of abundance within you. You've created it and have an endless supply of this essence. So, you become more generous with your smiles, your compliments, your acts of kindness. Soon, you'll naturally become more likeable, even if you're already amazing. People will start responding more positively toward you. You begin to attract people and opportunities into your life that support your growth. That's the beauty of life; it often has a more magnificent plan waiting to unfold if you let it.

CASE STUDY: Dorothy's Garden Blooms

Dorothy, a woman in her sixties, came to my office for health issues, anxiety, and emotional distress. She'd been diagnosed with an autoimmune disorder that had her distressed and rattled. She was experiencing symptoms of excessive sweating, inflammation, insomnia, and "brain fog." Dorothy had three children, was divorced, and had changed her career pathways a few times. She was a lovely woman who seemed quite self-aware. She was willing to understand herself better and had a will to improve. She had been left by her husband many years ago and had given up on love. Her children were grown up and living overseas. She felt lonely and tired but was optimistic enough to heal. She expressed feeling like her body was "attacking" her. She was "fed up" with her symptoms and was feeling "disgusting" with the excessive sweating. She also spoke about being "totally fed up with my stupid brain; I can't get out of this fog."

I introduced the idea of thinking about her "broken" body parts as child parts. I asked her "What would it be like if you spoke to the sweatiness and told that child part IT was 'disgusting'? How do you think the child would react?" She was somewhat surprised to think of it in that way. She said, "Well, I guess the child would get pretty upset and angry." No surprises there. How would a child respond if she gets told she is disgusting regularly? It would probably retaliate with anger and withdraw with sadness. I got her to think of her body reacting like this. Sometimes, it would feel angry and inflamed. Other times, it would feel withdrawn and dysfunctional. She began to have a greater understanding of what was happening within her body. She became aware of how she spoke to her body. How anger and sadness would compromise her immune system. Dorothy realized she was producing chemicals that were making her body sick.

Hypnosis allowed her go inward to heal. Gratitude also played a big role in her healing process. She would acknowledge her body and all the wonderful things her body does regularly for her. All the old wounds of abandonment, loneliness, rejection started to heal. Soon, she started a process of forgiveness, healing, and love. Not surprisingly, her symptoms began to diminish. She not only started to heal and feel better, she started to love. She began to love her body, love her life, and the people in it even more. She got energy back, and Dorothy began to love her garden.

She'd had a fantasy of growing her own plants and vegetables but never got around to it. She started talking to her plants, telling them how beautiful they looked. She talked to the little bugs around them and thanked them for the role they played. This slowly became a place of love for her. She'd curiously go outside and check if the spider from the fiddle leaf plant was still there. Suddenly she felt there was a world around her. She felt accompanied by all these little insects and plants. Dorothy poured her care and attention on them. She no longer was obsessed with all the bits in her body not working the way she wanted them to. She ended up constructing such a beautiful garden that she began to fulfil her dream. Growing her own veggies gave her a huge sense of joy. She was no longer angry every time her children called, telling them off first thing for not having called all week. Not surprisingly, they didn't call her too often. Every time she'd criticise them and tell them how lonely and abandoned she felt, that just created heaviness and guilt in them. Now, she had something to share. She wasn't consumed by her negativity. Now, when her children would call, she'd share her stories of her plants; they heard joy in her voice. Now, she was the one cutting the conversations short because she had things to do.

She dedicated daily time to self-hypnosis and meditation. She started to speak lovingly to her inner child, to her organs, her body, thanking her organs for all the wonderful work they do. She apologized for having ignored them for sixty years, only paying attention when she was in pain or her organs weren't working. She asked her inner child for forgiveness. The little girl inside had not been allowed to come out and play. The inner child had not been allowed to be creative, notice little spiders in the plants and rainbows in the sky. As she blossomed, so did her garden. She had grown so many veggies that she would often take them to people's homes as gifts. Dorothy started nourishing her body with homegrown nutritious foods. Her vitality increased as her symptoms continued to decrease. Her good days were outnumbering her bad days.

On occasions, she'd have a spike in symptoms. Instead of feeling angry at her body, she'd do her self-hypnosis and reframe her mind. She reminded herself of her body's own healing mechanism. The days she was lethargic, no energy to get up, she allowed herself to rest. She didn't push her body. She spoke to her plants and spiders from her bedroom window. She'd send them love and gratitude for looking after her as she rested in bed. Dorothy's entire world began to change. She created new relationships within herself and around her. She changed her mindset; her focus of attention shifted. Life started to love her back. Her children were more present. Her friends were more appreciative of her veggie gifts, more caring. She changed the frequency and vibration of her being. By doing this, she changed the frequency and vibration of all those around her. Later on, Sandy, one of her friends, introduced her to Tom, a friend who had an organic farm. Sandy had made lunch one day and had sprinkled fresh herbs on the food. Dorothy had given her these herbs. Tom was delighted at the taste of the herbs. Tom asked Dorothy if she wanted to be involved in his organic farm. She was fascinated; she started to study organic farming practices. A whole new world opened up for her. She said to me "I feel more alive now, more loved, and more satisfied with who I am at the age of sixty-three than I ever have my entire life."

The beauty of Dorothy's story is one of healing not only her physical body but also her spirit. She got on top of most of her symptoms and learned to manage the rest positively. Her quality of life definitely improved. She healed her body and transformed her mind. She found love within herself, within her "failing" body. She found love within her home environment. The moment she stepped out of anger and into forgiveness and love, she started to heal. And that's what she did; she loved it out of her body.

Exercise 1:

- Write down how you speak to your body and about your body:
    - ○ "I hate the way I look."
    - ○ "I can't stand my nose."
    - ○ "I can't get wet; I'll get sick."
    - ○ "I'm always so tired in the mornings."
    - ○ "My mind is so hectic."
- What feelings arise with these statements?
    - ○ Do you feel anxious and tense in your chest?
    - ○ Do feel sadness, anger, guilt?
    - ○ Do you feel unworthy?
- Where in your body are you feeling these emotions and sensations?
    - ○ Scan your body and see where you are holding tension.
    - ○ Are there any parts that feel pain or discomfort?
    - ○ Are you drawn to parts of your body as you think about this?
- Notice your breathing.
    - ○ How has your breathing changed?
    - ○ Do you feel more relaxed or tight in your chest?
- Take some time to write these reflections down in a journal.
- Close your eyes.
- Put a hand on your chest and the other on your abdomen.
- Take three long deep breaths.
- Expand your abdomen as you breathe and open up your chest.
- Inhale through your nose.
- Slowly exhale through your mouth.

- Do this again and repeat the following statements in your mind:
  - ○ "I am safe in my body."
  - ○ "I feel calm in my body."
  - ○ "My body is healthy and strong."
  - ○ "I trust my body."
  - ○ "I love my body."

Exercise 2:

- Focus on a spot on the wall in front of you.
- Take a deep breath.
- Have the intention of releasing all the negative feelings about your body.
- Take another deep breath and close your eyes.
- Focus on the top of your head and fill your body with a nice golden light from head to toe.
- Feel this light relaxing your muscles and your mind.
- Now imagine you are in front of a fire; notice the flames, the colors, and the warmth.
- Imagine writing down all the negative thoughts and feelings about your body on a piece of paper.
- Imagine scrunching up that piece of paper and throwing it into the fire.
- Watch it burn, released permanently out of your mind, out of your body, out of your life.
- Now take a deep breath and feel the sense of relaxation expanding through your body, a sense of relief.
- Visualize drinking a glass of water, letting the water cleanse you and revitalize you.
- Feel your mind is clear; ready to have empowering, confident, healthy, and loving programs installed.
- Take a deep breath. As your body expands with the inhaled air, your cells fill with confidence, health, and vitality. Feel your cells expanding with love.
- Do this breathing three times.
- Now say to yourself: "I am empowered, I am confident, I am healthy, I am loved." Repeat this three times.

- Now to finish off this exercise grab a piece of paper and write this down:
  - I am empowered, I am confident, I am healthy, I am loved
  - I feel empowered, I feel confident, I feel healthy, I feel loved
  - It is safe to feel empowered, confident, healthy, and loved
  - My life represents empowerment, confidence, health and love in every aspect
- Say it out loud three times.
- Get into the habit of doing this regularly (daily if you can).
- Stress accumulates daily, release it frequently.

Today I forgive you.
I forgive all you have done to me and all you have failed
to do.
I forgive you with all my heart as I know my heart yearns
to heal and sing again.
I forgive you because I can, because I know that
forgiveness will heal me and you.
Forgiveness is my strength, to carry on living as if I'd
never been hurt,
Living as if I'd never been let down.
Today I forgive you because I want to live a life filled
with love and joy.
I forgive you because it makes my heart lighter and your
spirit brighter.
I don't need to understand the 'whys' of your actions,
I just need to know my heart yearns to be filled with
kindness and joy, not hate or resentment.
I let go and let life in.

Kali

CHAPTER 4

FORGIVENESS WINS

That's Rubbish! Phnom Penh, Cambodia 2005

It was a hot humid day in the city of Phnom Penh in the summer of 2005. I was volunteering in an orphanage just out of the city. I had decided to visit remote villages in Cambodia during my time off. This particular "village" was to be one of the most memorable, for all the wrong reasons. Off I went on the moto-taxi to the local market to stock up on fresh fruits to take with me. I arrived at the "village" located alongside the Phnom Penh rubbish tip just out of town. I was covered from head to toe as I walked up toward the village. The stench of the rotting rubbish was nauseating. As I stepped through hills of rubbish to get through, I noticed that sometimes I couldn't see what I was stepping on, covered in black masses of flies. My feet would sink into the rubbish a little and my stomach turned. It was confronting on so many levels.

I had my eye on my goal, the village at the top. There were trucks in the distance dumping rubbish. Hills of burning rubbish around me on the other side. I was carrying bags of fruit; I would exchange food for stories and photographs. I pushed through the rubbish; it was my least favourite of hikes. I could see some locals sitting on woven mats on the top of one of the hills. I walked up the enormous hill of rotting rubbish trying not to slip or touch anything. I finally got there and in my limited Khmer language I greeted them. I asked for permission to join and sit by their side. I offered some fruit as my first way of acknowledging their presence and to connect with them. Their faces lit up and appreciation beamed from their weary eyes. We had conversations in my broken Khmer and their broken English. There is something so beautiful about these "broken" dialogues, something so innocent. They told me they lived and worked in the rubbish tip. Sorting the rubbish out, burning the rest. In the hill next to us, you could see black smoke slowly burning a big hill of rubbish.

They informed me that there was a small village on the other side with some houses where they lived. They told me that most of the workers in the rubbish tip live in that little community. They were so friendly and kind to me, I had a beautiful moment of just appreciating this connection. For a moment I forgot I was sitting on top of a hill of rotting rubbish. I was unaware of the stench at times and my mind focused on the sweet smell of the mandarin peels that lay next to us. My eyes were engaged in their beautiful faces with their high cheek bones and gorgeous tan skin. Khmer people have the most beautiful smiles. Their whole face lights up with a sense of tenderness. It never ceases to amaze me how easily people smile in challenging situations. Nevertheless, you could see deep sadness in their eyes. After the smiles were gone, there is still a very deep sense of heartbreak in their gaze. Khmer people have endured so much in such recent times. Their trauma is still alive; nevertheless, they beam with love. They insisted I go there and take the rest of the fresh fruit to the children in their village. They kindly pointed me in the right direction and showed me the way down to the village.

I walked down the rubbish hill, once again trying not to slip and arrived at the village with the fruit and my camera. Like most of these little villages, children are playing around, chasing dogs, chickens, and pigs. When they see a foreigner, they gather in awe and fear. They stop and look; some nervously laugh, covering their cute little faces while others run away and cry. These children were covered in soot and dirt, I had to hold back my disbelief and tears. As they gathered around me, I gave out mandarins and lychees. They eagerly bit into the juicy fruits. In front of me was a child only two years old or so. He was covered in so much dirt that as the mandarin juice dripped down his chin, it left a line. My eyes grew wide in disbelief as I watched the white mark clearing away the dark dirt. I spent some time among the villagers, having more broken conversations. I asked for permission to photograph them and they gladly accepted. I stayed for some time and played games with the children. The food ran out quickly. I went back out to the local market and took more food back to the village. I held it together in front of them; on the inside, my heart was breaking. My tears were welling up, and my stomach was tight. I couldn't understand how a world I cherished so much could let this happen to other people. At the same time, I was having a beautiful time with these kids and people.

As I made my way back into the city on the back of the moto-taxi, I had tears streaming down my cheeks. I couldn't hold them back any longer. The ride home felt interminable. When I finally got home, I cleaned up and cried in despair. I was heartbroken and angry at the world. I sat on the balcony trying to process what I had just witnessed. It was a balmy summer afternoon; I sat and watched the sky change colors. The children below me were playing in the streets. You could hear laughter and vendors walking by. I felt joy to see children happily playing, but I felt an uneasiness inside me. I was disturbed; I couldn't shake off the images in my mind. I had so many questions, so much anger, such deep sadness, and no one nearby to talk to.

After several hours of staring at the sky, I got up and walked down to the local telecommunications shop. This was a time before everyone had a mobile phone with Internet or, at least, I didn't. You still went to the Internet shop and dialed up to get online. I remember trying to compose myself before calling home. I was so upset, I didn't want my parents to take a call with a sobbing daughter on the other end, as they would worry. I got connected and after making sure they knew I was well and okay, I let the flood gates of tears open. I was a sobbing mess overcome with awkward hiccups. I remember saying to my parents, "How can the world not know about what is going on here, and if they do, how come nobody does anything?" I sobbed on the phone to my parents for what seemed like an eternity.

I was merely a young university student at the time. I couldn't do much more than provide food, medical supplies, books, toys, and pencils. I would use my photographs to hold fundraising exhibitions, to raise awareness and share stories through images. But I felt helpless, I felt disgusted at humanity, I felt angry. I felt tears of sadness and injustice running through me. To me, it was just utterly unacceptable to live in such an unjust world. A world that allows our fellow brothers and sisters to live in mountains of rotting rubbish. It was wrong on so many levels. I even felt angry with the people in Cambodia who were indifferent to these people.

I felt resentment toward those who had more. The children and adults at the orphanage where privileged compared to these people. I simply could not get my head around this. I was angry at myself for not doing more earlier; I was angry at my privileged life and my luxuries. It was a lot to digest for a young twenty-five-year-old. My parents lovingly held my tears and my pain over the phone as best they could. They encouraged me to remember why I was there, to learn, to have experiences, and to serve at the orphanage.

I realized that if I were going to be of service, I couldn't hold this rage. I couldn't hold this anger inside me that made me feel contempt toward everyone who wasn't actively doing something about this. That was just pointless. I knew my feelings and view were distorted and I was being reactive. I had to find a way of forgiving others and myself for not having done anything sooner. I was triggered and angry and exhausted by what I had witnessed. I knew I had to overcome my emotions. I had to keep my focus on my intention. My intention was to plant seeds of hope in children, seeds that good people do exist, that allow children to grow up feeling worthy with the right to have a safe and loving life. I wanted to plant seeds that education can be fun. I wanted to show these beautiful little souls that being in an orphanage did not make them any less lovable for a second. I had to pull myself together and go back to a mentality of love and service. I needed to serve the orphanage and the NGOs I was working with.

I got some guidance from my support workers. I processed some of these feelings. I found a way of allowing this anger to inspire me to spread awareness. I journaled and wrote about my experiences; I wrote to family and friends in Australia to raise funds. I continued to work at the orphanage and to love the children and staff. I arrived every day with my best hat on. The happiest of smiles, energized and ready to share my knowledge, ready to share my resources, and, most of all, to share my heart with all these sweet little souls. I was greeted by children running up to me happily yelling out, "Hello, Kali" as I arrived at the gates of the orphanage so excited every morning. So, my love affair with Cambodia continued for a period of five years, going back every summer to be of service. I still don't feel I did enough; I still feel so much more can be done. I have come to terms with that. I have accepted that you do your best in any given situation. I hold such deep love for that time in my life and all the people I worked and lived with. I understood that holding resentment toward anyone, regardless who they are, is unhealthy. So, I had to forgive, be at peace with my efforts, and let it go.

As Einstein said, "You can't solve the problem at the same level it was created." You have to rise above it, overcome yourself; I had a lot of work to do. Little did I know Cambodia would be my training ground for some of this forgiveness journey.

I Forgive You

Forgiveness is a timeless concept, one that holds sacred worth in most cultures. It is seen as a gesture that embodies compassion, love, and hope; it heals the self and those around you. Forgiveness is the act of making a conscious and wilful decision that surrenders feelings of blame, vengeance, hurt, fear, anger, and betrayal toward the offender (Brannan et al., 2016). Forgiveness allows you to let go of the emotions caused by someone's wrongdoing toward you. It also plays a role when you need to forgive a wrongdoing on your part. The great English poet Alexander Pope spoke of forgiveness as a divine aspect within us all, "To err is human; to forgive, divine." Many other great people in history have spoken of the power of forgiveness. We are all guilty of some wrongdoing.

We have all made mistakes in our pasts; own your mistakes but keep moving forwards.

Oftentimes, forgiveness is seen as a weakness. I encourage you to befriend forgiveness; it is a powerful quality to develop. Practicing forgiveness can actually be a protective mechanism against stress (Nussbaum, 2016). Failing to forgive can create rumination and a series of negative thought patterns that quickly snowball into strong unhealthy emotions such as hate, revenge, and anger. When you are able to forgive, you are allowing the body to let go of some of those stress-inducing emotions. Forgiveness promotes prosocial behaviors; this strengthens the relationships you have with others. By now, you would have noticed how important it is to be on top of your emotions, the importance of keeping the peace in your relationships and within yourself. Forgiveness plays an important role in being able to undertake all of those things. When you are able to make peace with something or someone, it can have significant impacts upon your health. When you forgive, you are able to release negative emotions associated with stress and chronic disease.

Neuroimaging studies have discovered that forgiveness improves brain function and your immune system (Ricciardi et al., 2013). They noticed that unforgiveness caused anger, impacting on immune function and increased cortisol levels. This creates a greater risk for cardiovascular disease to occur. When they assessed brains of people who embraced forgiveness, they noticed an increase in stimulation of the areas of the brain that are calming. This allowed the parasympathetic nervous system to relax the entire body. These people experienced more compassion, love, peace, gratitude, and happiness. They had lower levels of anxiety, lower depressive traits, and higher immune functioning. It's pretty amazing that forgiving someone or something can have such a significant impact on your body. Similar effects have been found when you forgive yourself.

Everyone makes mistakes; it's part of life and human nature. Forgiveness allows you to be more understanding. It gives you the ability to adapt to situations and to let go; this can be quite liberating. It pays to forgive; isn't that the whole point of life? To love and be loved? If forgiveness leads to love, and love is your ultimate goal, then let's relax a little and forgive more easily.

When you work from a space of love, forgiveness is definitely necessary. Everyone has something to forgive. You can forgive others, forgive yourself, and forgive life circumstances. I had a hell of a lot to forgive; I wouldn't be who I am today if forgiveness hadn't played a significant role in my life. Forgiveness is a very personal experience; it can be challenging at times, but the healing qualities are worth it. It helps heal your body, your psyche, and your relationship with others.

Sometimes, you might feel that a person or situation doesn't deserve forgiveness. Trouble is, it damages you to hold onto the anger, the grudges, the hurt. All the energy you hold onto with all the festering feelings creates a barrier that doesn't let you be at peace. Not only that, but the ongoing hurt and damage you experience by not forgiving means the event continues to harm you long after it's over. The freedom that forgiveness gives you is the real gift. When you forgive, you are activating your ability to step into the practice of being love. This is a really valuable quality to develop, being able to embody love. Facing situations from a space of love, you want to be conscious and aware of who you are being in each moment, choosing love, choosing kindness, choosing to be the better person. Just imagine how your life would unfold if you could love more openly and let go more easily.

I'm not saying let other people walk all over you. I'm saying be strong in your boundaries but make sure they come from a place of love. Lead with love; show everyone around you that you will not let hurtful experiences control you. A wonderful concept in the book, *Conversations with God*, by Neale Donald Walsh is the concept of love being a person. If love were a person, and love were faced with the situation you're facing, what would love do? Let's say it's an argument with your partner who has been unreasonable and taking things out on you. Ask yourself, what would love do in this situation? Some people would react and say, "It's unfair; my partner is being unreasonable and not acknowledging my efforts." Now, all those things might be valid, but what would LOVE do? Love would understand, love would forgive, love would give your partner some space. My question to you is what outcome would you like? If you love and value the relationship, you're most likely to want to solve the issue. Meet each other from a greater level of understanding. Learn to rise above situations that hurt; allow that divine source within you to take over as you let go and forgive. It doesn't matter if you're always the "bigger person." Being the bigger person in a situation makes you stronger, more valuable, and creates a strong sense of self. This means you understand why others act in hurtful ways, and you understand that you are not defined by their actions. Choose to forgive; choose love. This concept of choosing love above all else can be challenging, I know. Ask yourself what you want; love will be the answer more than you think. If you're willing to stay in a good relationship or walk away from a toxic one, then the answer is ALWAYS to be love. Love yourself enough to forgive.

"To err is human; to forgive, divine"
—Alexander Pope

Be Love

Your ultimate goal is to have a life filled with joy, a life that is fulfilling, that is rich with experiences adorned with blissful feelings, to feel a true sense of love for life, a love for yourself and your communities and to feel you've lived a life worth living. I'd like you to develop an understanding of the concept of unconditional love. Think about that for a moment; what does unconditional love mean to you? Unconditional means it has no limitations; it has no list of terms and conditions you need to sign off on. You don't love your dog only when she does what you tell her to do; you love your dog even when she chews up your leather boots, as my dog Lola did when I was a grumpy teenager. You get upset, you put consequences in place, then you let it go and move on. Being upset about it for longer won't change the fact the dog chewed up your favorite leather boots. It's easier with animals and much more challenging to apply to humans but necessary.

Everyone needs to find healthy ways of understanding and forgiving each other. Think about children for a moment. If you were conditional with them, you'd send them back after the first time they threw food at you, the first time they drew on the walls or kicked you in a fit of rage. But you don't hold a grudge; you understand they're learning how to navigate through life and their emotions. They're expressing their creativity with crayons on your freshly painted walls. They're playing with food and textures, testing your patience and boundaries. You deal with the situation, understanding they are learning and exploring; you are unconditional with them, most of the time. They will yell at you, kick you, throw things, laugh, and cry. You don't dialogue with them, getting them to understand all the hard work you've done. When they're upset, you scoop them up, give them a cuddle, and help them settle down. Afterwards, once they've settled, then you might have a chat about what's going on. Why don't people do this with adults? Adults are just children in big bodies. Adults carry the same needs and wants as a child: to be safe, loved, and acknowledged. The reason is you put high expectations on one another; you expect others to meet your needs and know what you're thinking and what you need. When you do this, unfortunately, you set yourself up to fail.

Think of your loved ones as small children who just need to be loved; it allows you to be more compassionate. You have love and kindness to give; so, share it. The only one you are doing a disservice to by not giving love is yourself. When you choose love most of the time, you begin to realize that you sweat the small stuff. You argue over silly things, and, at the end of the day, so much energy is wasted on things that truly don't matter. From a biological perspective, forgiveness heals your body; it heals your heart. You often store deep pain and hurt in your heart; think of how people express having a heartache or a broken heart. The heart has been said to be the most significant organ in your body. Not only is it a sign of life to have a healthy heart but it's the organ that creates the largest energetic field around you. The Heart Math Institute has studied this extensively. A happy heart is a powerful heart; it is the most valuable aspect of the human condition. When you forgive, you release energy that may be stuck or stagnant in your heart space. As your heart begins to heal, you create greater harmony in the heart-brain connection. This is important as it allows the body to go into a more balanced sense of synchronicity. You feel more "at ease" in your body. Your natural state is one of love and harmony. So, it is only natural that the body feels so good when you can let things go. It's like the wonderful feeling of making up with someone after a fight.

Forgiveness does wonders for your body, partially because it allows you to feel healing emotions. Emotions that heal change the frequency of your body. Considerable scientific research shows health benefits of these high frequency emotions (Pert, 1997). These emotions not only feel good but also change your body; love and forgiveness lower blood pressure, increase immune function, lower cholesterol, and decrease cortisol. How incredible is that? Your body is the most amazing pharmacy in the world! I want you to think about your emotions as chemical architects in your body. You are designing how and what you want to feel. When I discuss this with patients and say, "If you thought of an angry fight or a stressed-out day as that taking a day away from your life every time it happens, would you do it regularly?" The answer is most often NO! But people do it all the time; they hold grudges or feel too proud to forgive or ask for forgiveness. You are constantly creating changes within your body. Those changes have the power to create illness or wellness, longevity or a death sentence. Think about forgiveness as building strength in your character. The wiser you are, the more easily you forgive. We are all humans; we all make mistakes. To forgive is to rise above those mistakes and not be held hostage by them. Do yourself a favor and let go. Your body will thank you; your spirit will sing.

> *"The weak can never forgive.*
> *Forgiveness is the attribute of the strong"*
> —Mahatma Gandhi

There has been no greater time in the history of humanity than right now to take full control of your life. In a time with information readily available, you can empower yourself enough to transform. It may even seem that self-actualization is within reach.

It may seem that your dreams might actually unfold in this life. It's at your fingertips, one step at a time, you can see it. It's the peak of the mountain and you're well on your way. Part of this is to climb up the mountain without holding onto the baggage from the past. The baggage from the past will only drag you down and slow your evolution. As a collective, everyone needs to let go of the stories that hold them back. Part of this process is honoring all that happened before you came to be. You can honor this without becoming a victim to it; that requires forgiving what was and wasn't done.

Such fast and competitive societies have been created that it's sometimes easy to forget who you are. Not long ago, your ancestors experienced real hardships: war, famine, and poverty. Now, everyone feels entitled to have and acquire more of everything, not to share more but to prove a point, to prove that they are worthy, that they have status and "power." At the end of the day, it's to prove they are good enough and worthy of being loved and accepted. Everything is so jam packed and busy now. Busyness has been glorified as well as rushing, comparing, competing. But what are we rushing to? To the grave, I think. There are many wonderful aspects of today's society, but this crazy sense of competition has created a separation that has harmed humanity. That also requires forgiving and rising above so you can move into other realities, more nourishing and life-supporting realities.

Social media has created a population of ego-driven competition where immediate gratification and disposable "everythings" is the norm. This creates superficiality, guilt, shame, and separation. It's difficult to get to the mountaintop with a heavy bag from the past, comparing your speed to others, checking your phone to see how many likes you got on your last social media post, and festering in anger over a friend's betrayal. I want you to see that all these things chain you to the past and limit your capacity to get where you want to go. Forgive yourself for getting sucked in to what society tells you that you should do and who you should be.

Now more than ever, people need to think and act as a collective for the good of all. The more you can forgive in general, the more you can share your love and feel connected to life. When you do this and you feel a greater connection to nature, the better the whole planet will be also. You see, the collective good for all always supports your growth. When you have an open, positive mind, a heart full of love, you create a stronger energy field around you. That energy field affects every person and space you engage with, influencing everything. So, if everyone is positively affecting each other, everyone thrives. The planet thrives and the Earth supports your growth. This is when you begin to truly feel you are part of a collective, everything is connected, and you are in constant relationship with nature. You have the power to heal yourself and, by doing so, heal others, nature, and the entire vibration of this magnificent planet you live on. Everything you do: your emotions, your vibration, how you speak, how you treat the person who serves you, the person you serve, the plants around you, it all has a ripple effect; it's all a big web. You are part of that web; you have great power to influence the world you live in. Create and become a loving "ripple effect" magnetically affecting the world you live in with blissful love.

Right Here Right Now

If you think of yourself as part of the universal web of life, you are essentially connected to all things. Everything unfolds in the present moment; everything else is just an idea of the past or the future. In this present moment, all realities can exist simultaneously at any given time (Moorjani, 2012). You can experience the past in the present by recalling a past memory and you can dream about the future in the present moment. By doing so, you bring your awareness of the past or the future into the present moment. You begin to understand the only thing that is real is the moment you are experiencing right here right now. Forgiving something that happened in the past allows you to let go of the hold it has on you, creating space to be present in the now! How you experience the present moment will ultimately determine your future moments to come.

If you change your perception of a negative event and step into love and forgiveness, that event no longer haunts you. You might even feel compassion for those who harmed you; this changes the perception you have of that person and the event. It's all about perception at the end of the day. This gives you choice to focus on things that matter. Remember that this can be an internal process; you don't necessarily need to verbally forgive another; you can do this in your heart and mind. You have a choice to forgive and let go. The beautiful thing about having choice is you can expand your mind. Your perception of life widens; you open up to new potentials and opportunities.

I want you to remember that your intention in life is to grow, to feel more love, to expand your experiences, and evolve. Letting go of past events allows you to free up space for you to have new ones. You can choose whatever you like. For example, you can choose to not be upset about an incident that happened. You can choose to imagine that there are many other ideas and thoughts you could be placing your attention on. Imagine for a moment you had the ability to look at the Universe like a space filled with infinite possibilities. Imagine millions of particles that you can reach and grab to create any experience you wish. You activate your internal vision when you do this; it stimulates your brain. You are just using your imagination by expanding your perception of life; you widen your experiences. Play with this concept with wonder; just play with the idea of creating anything you desire. This activates your ability to visualize and imagine; this is a wonderful thing for your brain. If you'd like to create a day with lots of laughter, imagine looking up to the expansive Universe and seeing that laughter unfolding; you might even start laughing or smiling. Play with this idea of visualizing and feeling magic unfolding.

I sometimes do this when I'm star gazing; there is something so magical about looking out onto a night sky that expands your mind. It reminds you of bigger things that go beyond what you experience in your mind daily. I'd love for you to start thinking that the more expansive your mind, the more parts of your brain working together. This activates novel thinking; this gets you outside of your head and your daily issues. It allows you to focus on more expansive aspects of life. Amuse yourself with these ideas; get creative. If you achieve nothing more than a few hours star gazing, I'm sure it'll be better spent than in front of your phone or TV. Magical things have happened to people when they play with the idea of creating experiences. Relate to life with curiosity like an enthusiastic scientist in his lab, excited to see if his formula works. Half the fun is in the process of the experiment, not just the outcome.

When you can start to look at life in this way, you begin to see that you have nothing to lose, nothing to prove. It's all just an experience. That sensation liberates you immensely. There is great freedom that comes with this, great liberation of all the socially imposed norms and structures. You begin to realize that not only can you walk to the beat of your own drum, you can dance to it, fly with it. Liberate yourself from the shackles of the ideas of society that were invented by people you have no affinity with. Let go of trying to impress others and stop doing what society tells you to do if it doesn't sit well with you. Give yourself permission to be you! Give yourself to whoever you choose to; express yourself however feels right to you. Let go of the need to follow socially acceptable norms created by old-fashioned conservative fools who made rules out of oppression, guilt, and shame. Have the courage to be you; be brave! Forgive the past; allow yourself to feel more love and make room for creative energy in your life. It'll do wonders for you.

CASE STUDY: Stacey Rises Above

Stacey is a forty-year-old woman who migrated to Australia in her twenties with her husband and children. Stacey presented for support with her fluctuating moods and complex trauma. She'd been working with me for a few months when she had to orchestrate a very stressful family event. Her mother was requested as a bone marrow donor to save her mother's brother who lived overseas. This was an emotionally charged and confronting incident for everyone involved. Stacey's mother was not in the best of health but she accepted to be the donor for her brother. They made the decision to travel to Africa for the procedure.

Stacey's relationship with her mother was turbulent; they lived in different cities and had very different lifestyles. Stacey actively participated in exercise, healthy eating, alternative therapies, meditation, and was doing her very best to construct a healthy life for herself. Her mother on the other side, dealt with her unresolved trauma by overworking, smoking, and drinking. As you can imagine, they were on polar opposite spectrums of awareness and self-care. So, when the time came to facilitate this epic journey, high levels of anxiety were being experienced by everyone. Stacey's mother had never returned to her home back in Africa since emigrating, and it was extremely confronting for her. Stacey had only stayed with her mother for a couple of days at a time at the most for many years. The prospect of having to stay together for an entire month was daunting for both of them. Not only were they going to be living together for a whole month but they would also be in a very stressful situation.

Stacey took all the leave from work she had accumulated to be a part of this trip. She had taken valuable time out of her life to do this with her mother and be a source of support for everyone. Although Stacey had a very strained relationship with her mother, she wanted to do this for her family. The days were long and exhausting. Stacey and her mother stayed in a family residence out of town and this would mean long drives to the hospital every day. Stacey drove around for her mother and other family members and supplied them with food, care, and nourishment. Each day melted into the next with endless tasks, and before she knew it, she was utterly exhausted. The environment triggered memories, negative flashbacks, unhealthy family dynamics, family guilt, shame, blame, jealousy. Family members wanted to see them, and they had no energy. Pressure was building up from every angle. It was a highly emotional experience for both Stacey and her mother.

One day, toward the end of the first week, Stacey and her mother had a massive blow up. Stacey's mother was reacting in the only way she knew how, which was blaming and victimizing, and this was Stacey's breaking point. Her mother was fuming with rage, blaming, attacking, and verbally abusing Stacey for anything and everything. Stacey had put all this time, effort, money, and had taken leave from work to do the right thing. She felt that her mother was unappreciative, out of line, and had no consideration for Stacey's needs. Stacey was unable to keep her calm, and the argument got heated, mainly around the unfair stance her mother was displaying. After the fight was over, Stacey decided to just do the practical things for her mother. She'd drive her to hospital every day, pick up relatives, do the shopping and just be there doing what she was there to do. Her and her mother never discussed the incident and they did this for another three weeks.

When Stacey returned and we started exploring the situation, there were big realizations. Stacey realized she was being confronted with childhood issues that were triggering trauma responses from her and her mother. Strong emotions had been deeply buried; she and her mother were walking time bombs waiting for the right conditions to blow up. The situation they faced brought these emotions to the surface in uncontrollable ways. Stacey realized that she wanted to be loved, appreciated, and respected by her mother. She wanted to be "mothered" when her mother was unable to do so. This is such a huge source of frustration and hurt for many. Going back home for her mother triggered emotions she had escaped from: shame, guilt, fear, and unworthiness. They had never returned to their African home town since they had emigrated until now, under stressful conditions. It was all too scary and confronting to expect anyone to act together, especially with underlying trauma. You see, when you're triggered and you're in survival mode, you feel everyone is out to get you. You're on edge, scared, not thinking straight. There is no room for considering other's needs when you're afraid of being attacked all the time. The slightest criticism will set you off. That's exactly what happened here.

Stacey was a smart woman; she'd done enough therapy to understand the situation, but she is also human, so she had needs that didn't get met. That hurts. She had to shut off her emotional needs and simply do the practical things to get through this ordeal. Once she was in a "safer" place, less triggered by her environment, she could then deal with the emotional aftermath. Out of threat, in a calmer space, Stacey was able to see things a little differently. After processing the hurts and emotions keeping her in stress mode, she crossed to the other side and found forgiveness. Forgiveness, self-compassion, and acceptance allowed her to reconnect to what she values most... her family. Stacey began to heal; she stepped away from being in survival mode that was causing her fatigue and low mood. It was too confronting for Stacey to consider forgiving her mother in real life, so we got creative and did this in hypnosis. As the mind doesn't know the difference between real or imagined, it allowed her to have the benefits of forgiveness without having to "deal" with her mom in real life. This ultimately changed the way she approached her mother, in a softer more understanding way, and she didn't feel as triggered by her as she did previously. This obviously impacting her mother's behavior toward Stacey. In order to forgive, she first needed to get out of survival mode, be the bigger person, and remind herself of what's important.

In hypnosis, Stacey and I were able to step into forgiveness exercises directed at her mother that were too challenging to do in real life. This is such a luxury, to be able to forgive someone in your mind and heart without having to be in the presence of that person. I guided Stacey to imagine she'd go to a healing space where she could feel safe and calm and release the feelings she held toward her mother. I got her to see it being released, feel it being released, and even hear the release. Hypnosis is a multisensory experience, so it's rich in sensations; the brain absorbs the suggestions and embeds the changes. Later on, we moved on to sending her mother love, sending love to all perpetrator and victim parts. All child parts holding onto wounds and traumas were beamed with forgiveness and love. After giving away all that loving energy, you can go into receiving, receiving all the love and care you didn't get. This can be reinforced with hypnotic suggestions for a more powerful experience.

Through hypnotic suggestions, I suggested she imagine that every time she sees or speaks to her mother, she can activate a sense of calmness. This helps the nervous system to not be immediately triggered into survival mode by the other person's presence. So, essentially, we are creating a new neural pathway in Stacey's brain that is in alignment to her values. Ultimately, that is improving her relationship with her mother. By doing this, she can act according to her values (family) and not be held captive by her trauma responses. She starts taking control back rather than reacting.

- Get out of survival mode; let go of negative emotions and calm your nervous system down.
- Be the bigger person; forgive.
- Remind yourself of what you value the most.
- Act in accordance to your values.

How To Use Your Mind To Heal

Now that you hopefully feel more empowered, you might need to figure out how to forgive and let go so you can let love be. You might be thinking, *How do I change my belief systems? How do I let go of my past experiences?* There are many ways of healing; I will primarily focus on hypnosis, visualization, and mindfulness techniques. As described earlier, hypnosis works in the awareness of your subconscious mind. This is where most of the programs that you run daily are stored. Hypnosis allows you to go in and clean out the programs, improve them and even create new ones. First, you need to check in with yourself and figure out what you're experiencing.

1. Get clear on what you're feeling, write your feelings down, and identify them.
2. Acknowledge you have those feelings, and notice where in your body you hold that sensation.
3. Breathe it out, do some good diaphragmatic breathing and release the tension held in your body. You self-soothe and calm your system down when you do this, preparing the right environment for healing to occur.
4. Imagine saying to yourself, "I forgive myself." Imagine saying, "I forgive you (name of the person)." If you feel comfortable saying this out loud, practice doing so.
5. Say out loud, "I forgive myself and others," "I willingly let go of all grudges," "It is safe for me to forgive."

Allow yourself to explore how this feels as a general practice. Take the time out to tune in to your body, calm it down, then willingly activate a feeling. When you do this, you are training your mind to feel more comfortable with emotions. This is a great practice, the more you can feel at ease experiencing emotions the better. You start to feel "safe" feeling sadness or anger, and it doesn't just throw you into fight/flight/freeze. When you can do this, you will be able to feel more in control when you are faced with a situation that triggers these feelings.

Closing your eyes and deep breathing relaxes you; when you relax, you change your brainwaves.

I want to remind you that when you are in a hypnotic state, you are in theta brainwave. This is a relaxed but aware state of consciousness. When your brain goes into these more relaxed states, it is stimulated in a different way than when you are awake, alert, and vigilant. By accessing different brainwaves, you are stimulating areas of the brain that otherwise lie dormant in your awake state.

This allows you to strengthen parts of your brain that guide you toward healing and greater awareness. By increasing your awareness and opening up to more positive feelings, you are on your way to self-actualization.

You essentially want to go through a process of stepping out of survival mode, releasing negative emotions, weakening negative neuro-associations. Then step into feelings that will calm the central nervous system down and send the message to the brain that you are safe. Then create new associations that are more loving, healing, and empowering.

Life will throw things at you; you will endure pain and suffering, and it will be confronting at times. How you pick yourself up and reconstruct yourself every time will be a great source of power. Knowing how to forgive yourself and life is a beautiful skill to master. Knowing how to get back up when life knocks you down, because it will, is mastering how you navigate through this journey. Every little step in the right direction counts; you're learning how to get there.

Combining Mind And Body For Healing

It has long been known that the mind impacts the body and the body influences the mind. When you go into a meditative state, you are gently blending these parts of you. Using your ability to focus on your breath, pay attention to your body and activate an image you merge your faculties with positive intent. When you calm and slow down your nervous system, your brain follows by slowing down the brainwaves. The calmer and "safer" your body and mind feel the more open you can be to meditate. Beginning to create the sense of peace of mind opens the door to healing within the realm of your subconscious mind. Dr Timothy McCall extensively explains how to use breathing and yoga techniques to calm your nervous system down and improve health (McCall, 2007). He describes that experiments with yogis show that controlling your breath allows you to control your mind.

Combination of breath, stretches, and poses unite all aspects of your body to access optimal states of well-being. You are learning to control your body through your mind and to influence your mind via your body. Meditation allows you to pay focused attention on a mantra (words) or a sensation (breath) while feeling grounded in your body. This is great practice. The more ways you can find of being with yourself in this manner, the more pleasant your internal environment will feel. These practices are wonderful for increasing brain health. Training your mind to focus on a sensation or a word strengthens your cognitive abilities. In a world that is full of distractions and over stimulation it's crucial to take time to focus your mind. Focus on your breath, your intention, and the emotions you wish to expand on; take some time away from your life to delight in your consciousness. Meditation is not about having a blank mind with no thoughts. It is about training yourself to improve your ability to focus on something with intent. Begin to train yourself to work in unison with your mind and body. They are beautiful allies working toward a common goal; guide them along the way with focused attention.

In my hypnosis retreats, I guide participants to use their mind to connect to their bodies. I prepare my participants by getting them to identify areas of their life they'd like to improve. They write down their healing intentions and take a moment to connect with these. Then I instruct them to calm their bodies down with deep breathing and relaxing sounds. We play with voice, chanting sounds, feeling the reverberation in their bodies. I run them through a process of connecting to their intentions and their bodies and creating calmness in their nervous system. This sets the scene for the mind to relax and open up for change to unfold. I then lead them through a thorough hypnosis session aimed at increasing relaxation, releasing negativity, and increasing empowering positive patterns. In this deep state, the brain is receptive to suggestions; the sounds create a soothing sensation and the body is relaxed in a supine position. These are the perfect ingredients to mold the mind and create powerful changes.

Some of the research I have conducted assessing mood pre- and post-hypnosis has shown significant improvements. Measured on a Likert scale from 1-10, 90% of participants reported an increase in positive mood post hypnosis. Of those 90%, the increase in positive mood was significant for 80% of participants, reporting a 30% increase in positive mood. The majority of people reported a positive effect either emotionally or physically, many of these changes remained for days and weeks after the event. This is encouraging and powerful to observe, when people come together with a willingness to experience and heal, wonderful things happen. I get so many emails and comments from participants saying they had the best night's sleep after the retreat, they hadn't felt that relaxed in years, and a pain in their body they had been struggling with suddenly vanished. The stories are endless. So many aspects of people's lives change by experiencing a different way of relating to the self. There is no doubt that when you combine the body's natural resources to calm it down and soothe its gentle being, you activate harmony. Add powerful intentions, active visualization, hypnotic suggestions, and trance-inducing sounds and you have a wonderful combination. This combination is like a magical elixir that activates your body's own healing mechanisms, your mind's empowering resources, strengthening the most beautiful aspects of your being.

Just gathering as a group with the intention to share a healing space with others that allows you to totally switch off is beneficial in its own right. The simple fact that deep breathing can slow and calm the central nervous system gives you the power to be in control of a sense of calmness and safety. These are all very important aspects of healing and living an empowered life. As I've mentioned before there is no room for creating a life of healing, love, and abundance when you are in survival mode. Use your body wisely to create the states you wish to experience more often. The more you do something with intention, emotion, and right action, the stronger you're making those neural pathways that will lead to feeling empowered.

Meditation and hypnosis not only feel good but they literally change your brain. Studies show that people who meditate have higher levels of activity in parts of their brain (prefrontal cortex) associated with higher levels of well-being. This includes happiness, immune function, mental flexibility, and positive attitude. These traits have been known to bring about greater resilience and less reactivity to the outside world, giving you greater control, better emotional regulation, and improved cognitive capacities, essentially making you happier, stronger, and smarter. Sounds pretty amazing to me!

Exercise:

- Find a spot to sit quietly.
- Put your hand on your heart.
- Take three deep breaths; tune in to your body.
- Say the following phrases to yourself silently:
  - "I acknowledge you."
  - "I honor you."
  - "I forgive you."
  - "I love you."
- Take another three deep breaths.
- Imagine a person you'd like to forgive or ask forgiveness from.
- Visualize the person in front of you.
- Repeat the statements, visualizing you are saying them to this person.
  - "I acknowledge you."
  - "I honor you."
  - "I forgive you."
  - "I love you."
- Now imagine you send them a beam of light from your heart, energetically forgiving or receiving forgiveness.
- Visualize feeling free from all negative feelings associated with this person.
- Imagine how it feels to have experienced forgiveness and tranquillity with this issue.
- Write down any insights you might have in a journal.

You are a field of boundless love.
You are divine, yet not fully blossomed.
You are always accompanied by
Universal love.
Look for it and you will find that
and so much more.

Kalí

CHAPTER 5

LOVE IS ALL THERE IS

Labor of Love, Elephant Conservation Park
Northern Thailand, 2006

It was a fresh morning at the beginning of a humid day. The day was about to unfold in the magnificent hills in Northern Thailand. I woke up early at the crack of dawn to the sounds of roosters crowing and animals rejoicing, welcoming and singing forth a beautiful new day.

I awkwardly climbed out of my mosquito-net-covered bed and got ready for the day. I could hear all the wildlife beginning to come alive. Their sounds, calls, and songs were waking everyone up. I looked outside the bathroom window and I could see beautiful vegetation, the sun rising, dogs running around, and a sense of excitement. I got ready for my day and started walking toward the main hub where I'd undertake my chore for the day. I could hear the elephants in the distance, and I was just bubbling with excitement.

As I walked through the muddy pathway, I felt alive, connected; I felt a huge sense of love toward this particular moment in time. I could feel the sun on my skin; it was warm in the freshness of the morning dew, and I felt so good to be there. I was at the Elephant Conservation Park led by Lek in northern Thailand.

On my way there I saw pigs, dogs, chickens, cows, and some horses, I joyfully said good morning to them all and felt a real sense of being alive. I had a spring in my step and a smile on my face.

I entered the thatched hut where I was allocated my task for the day. I was to husk corn for the elephants. I was shown to my husking spot and off to work I went. There were literally tons of corn to be husked. I sat there with some other lovely volunteers and I just went to work. I was so honored and felt such a huge sense of pride in merely husking corn, as I knew it was to feed the elephants. I have always been very fond of elephants; they have always inspired me, and I have felt a deep connection to them since I was a little girl. So, this was truly a dream come true. As I husked and started to listen to conversations around me, I noticed some people complaining about the task. I observed how my mind was deeply connected to the elephants; this corn I was husking was for them, so it gave me great joy to do this. I felt so wonderful to be part of the process of caring for them that it didn't feel like a chore at all. I was beaming and glowing the whole time and gladly husked for hours. After a while, my hands were sore, and I'm sure I'd cut myself here or there a few times. As you can imagine, elephants eat quite a bit, so we needed buckets and buckets of corn husked. I could feel the discomfort in my hands, but it never went through my mind to stop; it was nothing major. I was there to serve the elephants, and this was part of it.

After the corn husking was completed, we'd do the morning rounds greeting the elephants. They were all so magnificently beautiful, displaying their distinct personalities. They'd extend their trunks out to say hello and most likely to see if you had food, such a beautiful way to greet an animal. Their trunks are so strong yet gentle and the texture of their skin is quite rough and wrinkled; it's quite a pleasant experience. As they reach out and make contact with you, their eyes follow you, looking you straight in the eyes, quite a fascinating experience to have. As you walk through the park enclosures you a begin to notice a lot of activity. It's quite an energizing sensation; I felt so alive. We'd take the elephants out for a morning walk along the reserve, what an awe-inspiring experience to walk next to such an animal. You walk along with their mahouts, their keepers. Some of these elephants have been rescued from logging and tourism, and many have endured traumatizing and inhumane practices. Baby elephants get "broken in" as a little calf to be trained for tricks in shows and to obey they owners. As they carry traumas, they need to be treated with a lot of caution, love, and respect.

Walking alongside such a magnificent animal is truly an honor. I walked alongside Jokia, one of the female elephants who was rescued. Jokia's journey, like many of the other elephants, is one of heartbreak and joy. Jokia had been a logging elephant in the Karen village of northern Thailand near the Burmese border. She experienced a horrible event when she lost her baby while working logging in the forest. Jokia wasn't allow to stop and properly give birth; they forced her to keep logging while in labor. After she'd given birth, they didn't allow her to check and bond with her baby. Jokia refused to work after this incident, and she was deliberately tortured and blinded by her owners. Obviously, the trauma this beautiful elephant suffered was just devastating. She now lives at the sanctuary and is safe and free. She will often go up to a log and stroke it with her trunk; the mahouts say that many of the elephants that have been used for logging do this. They have this reminder of their logging days and will often feel and sense the logs on the ground and sway.

Although Jokia is blind in both eyes, she can still walk and do most things other elephants can do. So, I walked alongside her, right next to her face with my hand on her cheek. As we walked, I would gently speak to her, describing the scenery; she was so gentle and beautiful. She would often stop to smell something or eat a delicious ball of tamarind fruit the mahouts give out. There was a palpable sense of magic being next to such a magnificent and imposing creature. She'd sometimes stop and kiss me with her trunk and wrap it around me, it was adorable and slightly scary at the same time. Their trunks are super strong, but she was kind and gentle with me. There seemed to be this innate sense of symbiosis awakened within me in a jungle with such a grandiose creature. A sense of connectedness that surpasses the complexity of language and cultural norms, pure divine heart-to-heart energy.

As we walked along the reserve, I felt so incredibly honored to be having this experience that nothing else mattered. I was totally immersed in this connection I'd established with this wonderful elephant. We then walked to the river. Elephants love their bath time; it's quite a fun activity to be part of. We walked along and there were many other elephants in the water with their mahouts and people helping to bathe them with buckets. Some elephants gently enter the water and let themselves be bathed by their carer. Others are a little more outrageous and roll around and splash in the river. It can be fun to watch but a dangerous experience if you're nearby, a gentle rolling over could literally squash you. Jokia enjoyed buckets of water splashed on her back, she'd fill her trunk with water and splash everyone. It's really quite marvellous how an elephant can be so playful. I was in the river, knee deep in the water pouring buckets of water, scrubbing her back, I was beside myself.

I can't begin to express how much elephants mean to me; I was just in awe of the beauty of this experience. I had a moment when I looked around and saw so many elephants bathing and people loving them, caring for them. It struck me as such an honorable interaction between man and animal. I developed a sense of being part of something really meaningful; it moved and inspired me. That was my first morning at the sanctuary, my heart overflowed with excitement and love. I had a true sense that we are here to serve, love, and support one another and play as elephants play.

I was so moved by this experience that a few years later, I took my dad and brother to the elephant sanctuary. I was reunited with Jokia; elephants have an exceptional memory. I introduced my family to her and we had a wonderful walk around the river. She'd scan me with her trunk, recognizing my scent, and then scan my dad and brother. She was generous with her rough trunk kisses and flapped her ears. It was such a heartfelt experience to share with my closest relatives. The way an animal responds to you when they recognize you is just beautiful. It makes me think there is something bigger going on here. We are all elephant lovers in our family, so this experience was delightful; it allowed us to bond in such a unique way. Their magic was now embedded in our hearts, filled with memories we'd shared. Our brains had now wired this experience, weaving it into the fabric of our family history. We are now connected at a deeper level, with Jokia in our hearts.

The Unlimited Nature Of Love

Love is boundless, unlimited, and everywhere in everything. Love is not limited to ideas related to a lover, a child, or a friendship. The experience of love can be found in husking corn and in walking along a muddy pathway. Love can be felt in bathing an elephant. The important aspect is that love is in everything all the time. Love is love; there is no limitation. Love makes the world go round. Temples have been built, songs written, and lives lost all in the name of love. Love is delicately woven into all aspects of human existence. The beauty is noticing subtle tones of love in everyday aspects of your own life. The more you love, the more you open yourself to love changing the biology of your body.

You may or may not be an animal person like I am; it doesn't matter because, as I said, love is love. It's all around you; in every nook and cranny you look into, you will find love. When you begin to realize this, you begin to notice it more easily. You can have multiple occasions on any given day to experience love. Part of it has to do with your attitude and perception of the situation. If I had been looking at husking corn as a chore I didn't want to do or something boring and meaningless, I would have had a different experience. My day would have unfolded with disappointed and negativity. I aligned to the bigger picture of why I was there: to serve the elephants. It wasn't about me and my needs and wants. It was about being there to give and serve. The moment I got out of the way and was purely focused on giving was when life gave me the most. There is real magic in being able to look at things in that way and allow life to love you back. More importantly, love boosts your body, your health, and your sense of well-being. It will literally change the chemistry in your body.

Love Buzz

Love boosts your immune system, improves cardiovascular health, decreases stress, and so much more; essentially love heals. Research in the areas of medicine, biology, and immunology all demonstrate health benefits of emotions such as love. Love plays a significant role in protective behaviors and healing in the body (Carter et al., 2013). Love not only reduces stress and illness but also promotes well-being and longevity. Some studies have found that love is so powerful that it influences the body's vital functions (Esch et al., 2005). The feeling of love acts as a natural anti-inflammatory and antioxidant. People "in love" have been studied showing significant changes in breathing rate, blood pressure, and increased mood.

Love stimulates parts of the brain associated with pleasure. These aspects are fundamental in creating long-lasting relationships. Gratitude and appreciation are close cousins that express love; this vitalizes the body and improves social interaction, strengthening relationships through positive reinforcement and reward. This creates greater pleasure and closeness in your interactions with others. When you feel love regularly, you are strengthening your mind and body and also your outer world. You are able to strengthen your relationships and the natural environment. Engaging with life in a light-hearted way with an open mind allows you to have more loving experiences.

Love also secretes dopamine, a pleasure activating chemical within the body. Dopamine is released when people do things that make them feel good. It reinforces the behaviors that are pleasurable. Dopamine has a significant impact upon your mood, boosting positive affect and attitude. Music, meditation, exercise, and good nutrition play significant roles in increasing and maintaining healthy levels of dopamine in your brain (Esch et al., 2005). Do more things in your life that are pleasurable!

The pleasure that love creates stimulates your brain and motivates you. This energizes you and generates a positive drive, encouraging greater compassion for yourself and others. All of these aspects of love are important forces that govern your own growth. Love bonds us. Love secretes oxytocin, the bonding hormone that strengthens attachment among people. In childbirth, large amounts of oxytocin are released; this supports the bonding between mother and child. From birth, you are chemically wired to bond; it's instilled in your DNA. This is essential for survival and evolution. Think about that for a moment; as humans, you need to bond to ensure survival. That means everyone needs one another; this is the importance of allowing yourself to forgive and love more. By doing this, you create stronger communities around you. There is huge power in that.

Humans are social creatures; we create emotional bonds to one another. These bonds strengthen attachment, creating a sense of safety and belonging. This sense of safety promotes well-being by reducing stress and establishing closeness. When you feel loved and supported, this helps to build trust and loyalty. These are essential parts of being well; when you are surrounded by positive bonds, you grow. In a trusting space, you can give rise to the luxury of contemplating purpose and meaning in your life. If you currently feel disconnected, this is the time to find a way to create stronger social bonds. Heal the wounds that form barriers around you and find ways of welcoming love into your life. Establish a strong bond to yourself and then slowly start constructing networks of support around you. Animals are a beautiful source of love that can create closeness. Experiencing closeness and support are sure steps in dreaming up conscious evolution.

When you connect to others from a place of love, you affect their energy field. It's the opposite of when you walk into a room right after someone has just had a fight and you can feel the tension; it feels dense. You can do the same but positively with love. The heart's energetic field is powerful; it has the ability to influence everything around you. When you are in a state of love, not only do you begin to feel better but you also begin to change the environment around you. You are in a constant relationship with the world around, affecting it, and being affected by it. You have an enormous power to create uplifting environments. This has significant implications for families, workplaces, public spaces, and how you engage with nature. You're emitting an energy that can be felt by all living things around you. When you walk into someone's home that has lively and joyful energy, you can literally "feel" it. That energy is being created all the time; be aware of what you're putting out there. Whenever you can, choose to feed the world with your inspiring energy.

Love is also present in sharing experiences, think of some of the fond memories you have. You will most likely bring up a few memories around food. Interestingly enough, oxytocin is secreted when you share food. Sharing food forms part of your social structures; it so happens that it nourishes the body in several ways. Doesn't food taste better when it's made with love? It feels good to make things filled with love and even better to share them with those you cherish. These experiences strengthen a sense of closeness, trust, and belonging (Carter et al., 2013). Most cultures around the world will gather for celebrations around food; there is joy in sharing that bonds people together.

Now you know that sharing food has a powerful impact on your sense of connectedness and your biology. Make it a habit to have experiences where you can share food with loved ones, especially if it's made with love and joy. You may not be the greatest cook; that's okay. Just gather some healthy ingredients and share them with someone you care about. It could even be the sharing of your favorite tea or fruit cut up nicely and made to look nice. The brain likes to see beauty; it will give you great joy when you do this. Take time to make things from scratch, slow down, get creative and share these experiences. It allows you to meet a basic need and access a state of connectedness. When used in a healthy way, sharing food (healthy, nourishing food) can be a real source of love.

Love Bonds
Love Heals the Body
Love Nourishes your Soul

Hypnotic Meditation Oozes Love

Imagine every time you have a blissful experience in meditation you secrete hormones that boosts your immune system and brain functioning. You create a sense of connectedness and awe. If this happened regularly, wouldn't you want to do it more often? Don't you want to have an awe-inspiring life? I get excited when I think that a simple activity like meditation or hypnosis can willingly flood my body with blissful chemicals. This makes me feel good. It makes my mind more alert; I feel a sense of peace and connectedness. It makes me feel so good that I don't let a day slip by without a good hypnosis or meditation session. If I'm in a bit of a dull mood, I dive straight in and come out feeling completely new. It impacts my whole day and how I engage with myself, my loved ones, my work, and my productivity. It energizes me and opens me up to new ideas; I'm driven, motivated, and excited by my life. It is the most accessible and effective thing you can do. This will not only fuel your body with vitality but also motivate your actions, increase prosocial behaviors, and make you feel blissed out! You will undoubtedly change the experience you are having. You become more magnetic, abundant, and exude vibrant energy.

You will find a link at the front of the book for you to access a hypnotic meditation I have especially created for you. Get in to the habit of using this hypnotic meditation daily or find a meditation that you like. Make time to activate your brain with feelings of wellness. Actively release all the negative thoughts and feelings you accumulate regularly. Making room for greater feelings, more expansive awareness, and more empowered mindset. As you do this, you will find that you will engage with yourself and the world in a more positive manner. You will start to change the biology of your body, reinforcing positive patterns of well-being.

How You Can Be Love When You're Fed Up

Imagine you've had a really difficult day, everything that could go wrong did go wrong. You're feeling frustrated, tired, and exhausted. You feel nobody understands you and life is a struggle. You normally go to an exercise class after work. You have a few options here.

Option 1

You come home and you have two hours before you have your exercise class to go to that evening. You've had enough, you don't want to be polite to anyone and just want to fall into a heap. You might revert to old patterns of comfort eating, watching a movie, and disconnecting from yourself. You will most likely be distracted, eat mindlessly, and dwell on your day. As a result, you decide not to go to your exercise class. What's the point anyways? You've already eaten all this junk food and you're moping; you're in your comfort zone. You are activating your brain's pleasure system with food, so you're feeling "good." This will strengthen emotional eating as a coping mechanism. This also creates a pattern of withdrawal; it will make you feel frustrated and isolated. You might start scrolling on your phone, looking for something else to engage in. You send a passive aggressive text message to a friend who hasn't replied to you for a few days. And you might just get yourself into an argument. Then you'll create a self-fulfilling prophecy. Your friend has reacted to your message and frustration rises; you're alone and feel lazy and off. You'll stay home, possibly self-soothe with some alcohol or more food, and your day ends on a poor note.

If this is the familiar pattern, it is what your brain will naturally revert to. Even if it is unhealthy, the brain will always take you to what's most familiar. This comes from a protection and survival space. In ancient times, when people lived in small tribes, it was dangerous to go out into unfamiliar territories. In today's world, the dangers are less life threatening with project deadlines, a nasty boss, ex-partner, too many bills, and not enough money. They all form part of modern-day society's "dangers." This is what triggers your fight/flight/freeze mechanism and sends your body into stress mode. Remember even if it is not life threatening, your brain will still react as if it were. Let's have a look and see what you could do differently to genuinely deal with the difficult day you have had.

Some important factors to consider when option 1 is happening:

- You're dwelling on your thoughts and feelings.
- You're more irritable and taking things personally.
- You start to think of all the reasons why you shouldn't go out.
- You start going through all the reasons (deadlines, lack of energy, ex-partner, money).
- You send a command to your brain to find proof of why you shouldn't go; the brain obeys.
- You start to feel sadness, loneliness, fear, rejection, hurt, pain.
- These emotions secrete chemicals in your brain that make your body feel tired and exhausted.
- Your brain looks for a "quick fix." The easiest known quick fix to activate the pleasure center is food. So, you eat overly sweet or salty food to make you "feel good."
- Any pain in your body begins to feel more exacerbated with cortisol rising. Tension increases and you are probably slumped on the couch with poor posture.
- You're defensive, ready to snap at someone or instigate a fight.
- In survival mode, you're ready to fight at the first sign of someone challenging you.

Option 2

You get home, have a bite to eat of something healthy, take a quick shower, and clean off the energy from the day. You put on a guided meditation, get comfortable with a blanket, and allow your mind to be taken to a healing space. You let go of the stress that has accumulated, take some deep breaths, and relax your body a bit. You now release the day's events, the stress, the negativity. You can find a bit more compassion for the people who aggravated you. Your entire body feels calmer, more settled, and safe by the end of the meditation. You're feeling more ready to socialize and go to your class. You go with a sense of excitement, knowing you'll see people you like and that it's a fun activity to do. You greet the people you know in an open friendly way. You feel a sense of joy to see others, a sense of belonging, and you enjoy your class. You get pleasure and stimulate your brain; you release stress. Now you leave the class with a sense of joy, a satisfaction that you've followed through with a positive action. You finish your day in a much more positive and nourishing way. You now feel a greater sense of belonging and connection to others. You feel accomplished to have shifted your mood entirely.

Some important aspects that are worth mentioning in option 2 of self-soothing:

- Feeding yourself with something small but nourishing can be a great way to ground yourself.
- Having a shower allows your body to feel warm; this, in itself, is a nourishing thing to do. Heat interrupts pain pathways, lowering tension and pain.
- Soaps with nice smells like vanilla, lavender, and sandalwood calm your nervous system. Smells stimulate your brain and have powerful effects on the body.
- Meditation music is often relaxing.
- With a calmer mindset, you can make better choices.

Option 3

You come home from work and you're struggling. You send a message to your neighbor or nearby friend to see if they are home. You're in luck. You have some leftover food you know she loves, so you make up a bowl and tell her you're coming over with some goodies. She's busy but happy to have you come over. You pop over with a pretty bowl of food, she welcomes you into her busy household, managing kids and bath time. You get some cuddles from the neighbor's kids and have a quick conversation with her. You share your day, debrief, and connect with her. She's grateful for the food you've taken over. She gives you some food she'd baked the day before too and you have a bit of a laugh and cry about life. Before you know it, you have to go back home. She encourages you to go to your class and says, "Just go; you'll feel better by the end of it." You take that push and quickly get ready to go out. You go to your class, you shake off the day, and feel better. You get back home and feel good to have been encouraged to go. You also feel supported by your friend.

Important aspects that supported your choices:

- You chose to give when you needed something; this gets you out of your head.
- You feel a sense of support and gratitude for the encouragement to go to your class.
- You send a text message to your friend, expressing gratitude.
- Your friend replies thanking you for the food you took over.
- You bond, you share, you grow. This strengthens your belief that you are supported.
- You are actively caring for yourself and those you love.

Love Can Be Expressed in So Many Ways
Self-Care Is Ultimate Love
When You Look After Yourself Well, You Can
Then Give and Be Open to Receiving
Self-Care Is Essential
Self-Care Is Love

What Are You Worth? You Are A Diamond On The Inside

What is self-worth and why do you self-harm? If you know your true worth, you're less likely to harm yourself. Self-harm can be in the form of negative thoughts, addictive behaviors, and poor self-care. I want you to think about how you value yourself. Do you value yourself based on external opinions? Do you value yourself based on your wealth and status? Do you value yourself based on your appearance? Are you worthy of friendships and love? Are you worthy of goodness in your life? Do you think you're a valuable person? Take a moment to reflect on some of these questions.

You are born as a diamond, the strongest clearest rock on Earth. Perfect, unique, and incredibly valuable just as you are. After birth, you roll onto water, you roll on some dirt, leaves, and flower petals. You go through life, accumulating layers around your precious diamond. Slowly, you build more and more layers. These layers sometimes seem like "junk." They are just life experiences. They shape you and form your outer façade. Some of these layers represent negative comments, bad experiences at home, or illness. Other layers are beautiful moments that coat you in flower petals. With a mixed bag of experiences, you continue to flow through life's journey. Life happens; you organically roll along.

When you're at the therapist's office, all you can see is the outside layer of dirt and junk. It's thick, it's heavy, and it often stinks! But that's not who you are. You've forgotten that you carry this precious diamond on the inside. That's your truth, your worth; it's unique and incredibly valuable. It has many facets to it; there is no other like it in the entire world. You have so many layers that make you who you are. Underneath all those layers of dirt, life's pain and suffering, there are layers of beautiful petals, love, and joy. You've got little gems stuck inside the muddy bits. The massive diamond in the middle is the essence of who you truly are. It is perfect just the way it is. You are perfect just the way you are; you might need to do a bit of cleaning up. You might need to wash off the dirt, and do a bit of work, but you do so, knowing that your essence is valuable.

You are remarkable, unlike anyone else, unique, and so worthy; you have just forgotten. Your worth is all covered up in layers of other people's beliefs, opinions, and things that have happened to you. That is not what defines you; what defines you is your essence, your ability to see what you carry deep within, even with all the layers of dirt on you. The process of healing and dealing with the "layers of dirt" you accumulate is a beautiful journey. Hypnosis is a wonderful tool that can facilitate the experience of peeling away the layers. Recognize you have baggage to deal with; it's a human condition. As you let go of the baggage, you uncover that diamond; it's waiting to come to the surface and shine.

Find what works best for you and start peeling those layers away. Realize that you have an incredible power deep within your mind; use it. Train your mind to think and feel empowered. Get to know yourself and have faith that you can and will change for the better. Use forgiveness, self-love, and kindness to aid you along the journey. Express a kind empowered attitude as you tend to these delicate parts within you. It will make all the difference. Get excited to go deep inside and let the diamond within you shine!

When you reconnect to your essence, your sense of worth, your life changes. The moment you change the perception of who you are, your life starts to change also. When you can begin to feel more worthy, you will act more worthy. This will emit an energy that will create a change in your environment, and this will change your experience. When you feel worthy, you begin to have more empowered thoughts. You begin to feel more positive sensations, and you allow yourself to dream. When you know how valuable you are, just because of who you are, you can't help but shine. Go on a journey of self-exploration and find that treasure, the real you. Long walks in nature can point you in the right direction.

"And now here is my secret, a very simple secret:
It is only with the heart that one can see rightly;
what is essential is invisible to the eye."
—The Little Prince

Pachamama Heals, Naturally

Being in nature inspires feelings of awe and wonder, a sense of oneness with all things. Nature provides momentary solitude and peace. It restores your natural connection to nature's harmony. This opens the door for transcendental experiences to occur. There is something truly magical about being in nature. It's almost like time stops; there is a sense of restored balance, a calmness about it. In this space, your mind expands, your heart goes into coherence. Nature provides the perfect environment for openness, creativity, connectedness. These sensations are conducive to health and vitality; they stimulate well-being in your body. In this natural state of harmony, you can open the door to accessing higher states of consciousness.

In the research I conducted exploring the effects of natural environment on mood, I made some valuable observations. One of these observations was situation selection, a person's ability to either approach or avoid a situation, place, or person to regulate emotions. Some people may avoid a situation that creates discomfort; others might go to a place that stimulates feelings of safety and peace. This is where the environment plays an important aspect in the role of mood regulation. Choosing environments that produce restorative effects is a powerful mood regulation skill. Nature does that beautifully.

Countless studies have explored the healing benefits of nature. Being in nature promotes positive moods, vitality, and a sense of connection. In Japan, forest bathing is widely practiced. This includes spending time in a forest, connecting to elements of nature, and absorbing the goodness. Forest bathing has shown to decrease stress, improve immune function, and regulate sleep, just to name a few (Li, 2008). When you are in nature, you are able to detach from the stressors of everyday life. You immerse yourself in the natural rhythm of Mother Earth. All of these aspects I'm sharing with you are about connecting. The more connected you feel to yourself, the more connected you'll feel in life. Do things in your life that allow you to grow a beautiful sense of love and connectedness. That alone will start the healing journey, and you will ultimately feel more empowered.

Whether you're at the beach watching a sunset or in a forest, there is no doubt you feel changed in some way. There is an instinctual sensation that rises to the surface when you are in natural settings. It is almost as if you arrive to a natural state you have forgotten about. You are part of nature; manmade cities have separated people from it. This separation creates a sense that you are out of balance. Days get filled with to-do lists, traffic, and so many daily pressures. People burst at the seams with stress; you push through until you crash and burn. You eagerly await your vacation time, to escape, to recharge. Masses of people evacuate the cities during vacation seasons in a mad race to get away. Most are driving away from their problems and stresses. Where are you driving to? Most likely a beautiful spot in nature. A place that provides solace, tranquillity, and rejuvenation, a spot where you can feel at ease again, relax, and enjoy. You arrive home. This is your natural state. It's like Pachamama awaits like a loving grandmother with open arms and a big smile. She is always there, ready to lovingly welcome you home.

Vacations in nature provide respite and rejuvenation for a variety of reasons. One of these is greater time in nature and removing yourself from stressors. Take a break from your life daily if you can. Leave your phone at home, go to the local park, and breathe in fresh air, sit by a tree, walk, read a book. Drive to the beach, have dinner with your family on a picnic blanket, feel the Earth beneath you. Find ways of incorporating this sense of balance and harmony nature provides. Do this regularly so you feel balanced more frequently. The more you can do this as part of your life routine, the greater your health and sense of connectedness.

Teach children around you the importance of respecting nature while enjoying it. Nature is there for you; allow its healing energies to be felt. It is so generous; it provides oxygen, shade, food, and shelter. Love it, respect it, and be one with it. The more you are able to be in natural settings, the more balanced you will feel. This will not only feel great but also protect you from stress and illness. It will make your daily experience of life more enriching. Your mind will be clearer, your thoughts calmer, and you'll enjoy life more. Nature is there to support you. Fresh air can revitalize you; a warm winter sun feels comforting. A dip in the ocean invigorates you and makes you feel alive. Walking on wet sand will ground you; it balances your body. Similarly, walking barefoot in a forest or nature reserve also grounds you. Create a conscious relationship with nature and feel a symbiotic flow unfold. There is a magical reason why millions of people around the world gather to watch a sunset. Some sort of magic unfolds as you watch the sun disappearing and the sky painted with colors. It is just magic; life is magic.

I strongly encourage you to make nature part of your life. Welcome her in, explore her, and love her. Organize gatherings in nature, watch the stars, feel the wind, bathe in the rivers. Every time you are immersed in it, you are helping your body to feel more balanced. It is available to everyone; make the most of it and protect her.

CASE STUDY: Alberto, a Chilean Story Of Addiction and Love

Alberto confidently walked into my office in Chile in a stylish outfit and slightly arrogant demeanor. A well-educated gregarious man in his fifties, he was there to give up smoking and to prove me wrong. He wanted to prove that he was not hypnotizable and that, surely, he wouldn't succeed, but he'd try anyway. He did have a strong sense of curiosity; he was open to hypnosis and, after all, he was there. His motivations for quitting smoking were related to medical complications he was experiencing. He also had a strong fear of death. He was in a lot of physical pain, facing surgery; he felt frustrated and tired. Alberto had big dreams, hopes, and aspirations and started to realize his health was slowing him down. At one point, it became clear to him that he needed to take care of himself. When I connected to his true purpose, a sense of self-care, I had something really good to work with. Oftentimes, the "referral reason" is rarely the actual reason someone seeks help. It's not just to "quit smoking" or stop emotional eating; it's a deep desire to connect with yourself from a place of love.

When Alberto realized this, he got excited; his guard came down and his demeanor softened. He ultimately wanted to have better health to live longer and enjoy his life. Cigarettes were costing him his health and his wealth. We explored what it would be like for him to truly love and respect his body. What would that look like? I asked him several questions:

How would you treat it?

How would you speak to it?

How would you feed it, move it, rest it?

How could you get to a space where your body was your best friend?

Alberto had never really thought about any of these concepts. He had just grown up and was on auto-pilot, unaware and disconnected. Alberto was moved by this idea. He felt connected to the essence of who he was for the very first time that he was overwhelmed by emotion. He had never had the opportunity to think of himself and his body in this way. During this process, Alberto connected to some childhood memories. He recalled losing his beloved grandfather to emphysema. Emotions rose to the surface and he wept at the thought of this memory. He vividly remembered his grandmother left a widow and the hardship this caused. It had created such a strong memory that he was petrified of doing it to his own family. Alberto was now so determined to give up smoking, he could not allow this to happen to him. He recognized he'd been careless and that he had created a negative relationship with his body for years. Overworking it, not sleeping enough, putting toxins in it, complaining when it didn't work. It never occurred to him to thank his body for anything. He never felt love for his body; the idea of this was as foreign as Russian to him. It just wasn't a concept he'd come across.

Alberto was now in touch with some confronting truths, and he wanted to improve. He didn't just want to give up smoking, he wanted to heal. He wanted to feel love and love his life. In hypnosis, Alberto connected to his body; he asked for forgiveness for all the years of abuse he'd put his body through. We dealt with the smoking addiction, emotions, and unhealthy habits. He let go of all those unwanted patterns that were making him sick. We worked on strengthening his body, activating the body's internal healing mechanisms, and instilling positive thought patterns that made him feel empowered and connected to himself. I got him to imagine how he wanted to live the rest of his life, healthy, confident, able bodied. He had a beautiful session and was blown away and humbled by the experience. He quit smoking that very same day.

He came back a few weeks later and he was a different person. He had implemented changes in every aspect of his life. He'd started walking daily, sleeping better, spending more time with his family; he was beaming. He was amazed by his changes; he felt a strong willpower to improve in every way he could. Obviously, he was ecstatic; he was a new man. He'd found a new sense of purpose and love for his life. He felt aligned to his values, his family, and his health. Alberto said to me, "I realize I have made excuses and run old stories that make me feel like a victim over and over in my mind. I now understand I can let that go and still be me. I feel like I have woken up from a fog and can see my life clearly." He decided to take full control of his life. He was empowered to create a much better reality for himself. Alberto expressed such a heartfelt sense of gratitude, it was palpable. He was so moved by his experience that it inspired me. It fueled my day with such reverence and love for this work; it moved me.

Love continues to do its amazing job of healing and paying it forward. It has a magical ripple effect, in an infectious kind of way. This is the beauty of love; when one person heals, it heals others too. Think about how lovely it is to know someone you love has overcome an illness, recovered or is feeling better. You feel the joy and gratitude too. When loves heals one person, they shine, and it gives others permission to do the same. And the ripple effect to continues to strengthen and transform.

Alberto's case to me is quite simple. A man who aligned to his purpose and values. He allowed himself to drop his guard and the façade he carried. He got out of survival mode and dropped the defensiveness. He connected to his emotions; he found his self-love. He took responsibility for his actions and his life. Alberto peeled away the layers that blinded him to see his essence, his love. He ultimately decided in one session he needed to change and be love.

Exercise 1

- Write a letter to yourself.
- Thank yourself for taking the time to do this.
- Describe what you love about yourself and why.
- Describe what you love about life.
- Write a list of whom you love and why?
- What do you love doing?
- What are some of your fondest memories and why?
- What is your favorite food?
- What is your favorite song?
- What smells, sounds, colors do you love?
- What would make you feel more loved?
- Imagine that event in detail, write all aspects of it.
  - Make a date with yourself, make your favorite food, put your favorite music on, wear your nicest clothes. Read yourself the letter. Promise yourself you will always look after and love yourself unconditionally.
  - Make a date night to do this every few months to review your life.
  - Make a date night with your loved ones once a month; actively value the people you care about.
  - Love and enjoy your life, let love in; you're worth it.

Exercise 2

- Write in your journal:
  - ○ I am filled with love and joy.
  - ○ I am totally at peace with myself.
  - ○ I accept and love myself unconditionally.
  - ○ I am complete.
  - ○ My mind is amazing; I am filled with loving thoughts and ideas.
  - ○ I am deeply loved and I feel loved.
  - ○ Wonderful opportunities open up for me easily and effortlessly.
  - ○ I shine and share my love with all those I value.
  - ○ Thank you for this life; So it is.

Today, I shall live with greatness,

I will choose my words to represent what I truly feel.

Today, I will use my time wisely,

I will do all I need to do,

I will slow down time to allow time for what I love,

I will stand strong honoring who I am.

My internal harmony grows more and more everyday

Kalí

CHAPTER 6

VALUES

Guided by The Masters—Mystical Valle Elqui, Chile 2012

I had left the ocean behind me as I entered the narrow Valle del Elqui. Dry arid mountains with soft hues of pinks and greys marveled us with the clearest of blue skies. Narrow roads curved along the mountain face with imposing rocky hills beside us. The Elqui river ran along the middle of the valley, a lifeline amidst the dry dusty landscape. Bright green vine terraces adorned the mountainous terrain. The bright blue sky is the clearest in the world; this is a mystical place. A perfect microclimate creates a fertile bubble for some of the best wine and pisco produced. Tiny adobe houses and small towns are scattered along the way. Round metallic structures on mountain tops glistened in the sunshine. Observatories are scattered everywhere; this is the ideal place for getting lost in the night sky. Avid stargazers and astronomers venture here for sparkling night skies.

Valle del Elqui is a place where time slows down; horses carry people to and from places, and nature keeps time. The stillness allows the crumbling rocks to be heard as they hit the water. The birdsongs echo through the valley. You're surrounded by a sense of magic, a sense that this place is guarded by the essence of the mountains. The mountains welcome and protect you as you gently venture into the core of the valley. I was on my way to Cochiguaz, a mystical little town right in the heart of the valley. I was traveling with my cousin Roberto, who is a mystical shaman in his own way. I had never been to Cochiguaz previously, so all of this was new to me.

Cochiguaz has a particularly special energy field; it is known as an enigmatic place in the Chilean desert. Roberto and I were on a mission to meditate and hike in this mystical place. We stayed near the river and we made ourselves at home there. We tuned in to the Earth, the water running by, the air, the stars. We made a fire that kept us warm in the cold desert night. The night sky put on a glowing performance; I sat and watched the stars shooting by like a firework show. The milky way was crystal clear, the new moon gracing the sky ever so slightly. There was definitely a feeling of mystical enchantment in the air. We took our time to connect to the land. Respects were paid to the land by forming a mandala. We used some of our own crystals, and rocks, leaves, and flowers we found nearby. We requested guidance from nature spirits and ancestors, showing we had come to explore with an open heart. We made our offering and let it go. This was the start of a series of events that astounds me to this day.

The next morning, we set out early for our adventure. The ever-present sun warmed us as we walked breathing in cold thin air. We found a spot and created a sacred space for our morning meditation. We sat in silence and meditated for some time. After meditation, we'd write down our thoughts or insights in our journals and then share them. When we compared notes, we realized we'd both received the exact same information. We wrote down specific directions to go to a sacred site. In our meditation visions we were told to go through a property to the left of the river, follow some old ruins until we arrived at a creek. We needed to cross the creek and continue walking up toward the top of the hill. At the top of the hill we'd find a circle of large white rocks that had been placed on this sacred site. Roberto had been channelling insights and information for a long time. I, on the other hand, felt like a bit of an apprentice. But I was open and had a thirst for knowledge and experiences.

We followed the guidance given to us. Walking down dusty roads accompanied by the imposing mountains. Trusting our visions, we walked with open hearts and open minds. We journeyed with a sense of childlike excitement. Out of nowhere a beautiful goddess-like cowgirl stopped in front of us on her horse. She had waist long honey brown hair, strong legs and a majestic presence. She asked if we were lost; I think Roberto was lost in her captivating beauty. We kindly declined directions and off she went. Her golden hair flowing in the wind disappeared in a cloud of dust. We had a bit of a chuckle and a choke in the dust puff she left behind.

We proceeded to walk; Roberto sensed something and had a hunch to turn left into a property. We walked into the property ascending into the base of the mountain. We came across a building that was in ruins; we knew we were heading in the right direction. I was excited and in slight disbelief. We continued to move upwards and forwards until we came across a little creek. We walked alongside it until we found a safe crossing. Although it wasn't extremely wide, the current was strong and had a feisty energy to it. I found some rocks perfectly scattered for us to step and jump across. The terrain got more and more steep on the other side of the creek, we hiked upwards and forwards. We had a gut feeling to go a certain way so we did, we must have walked for about thirty minutes or so on an incline. In the distance you could see an unusual patch of dense forest-like vegetation. As we walked through it, we felt a sense of tranquillity. All the sounds of nature could be heard. I emerged on the other side of this little enchanted forest and stopped in my tracks. I couldn't believe it; I excitedly whispered to Roberto to hurry up. We had found a flat plateau with huge white rocks perfectly placed in a circular shape. Roberto and I looked at each other and got goose-bumps.

We allowed some time to process the preciseness of the guidance we'd envisaged. As I mentioned before, neither of us were familiar with this place, so it was somewhat mind blowing. There was a sense of surprise but also a sense of "well of course it's all perfectly guided." We did what we knew best, connect to the Earth and meditate. We used some hypnotic techniques to enter a trance. At times, a dialogue would unfold in which Roberto would channel messages through. In that sacred space, we felt a sense of being held, welcomed, and accompanied. We completely lost track of time in a trance state. Roberto and I would "compare notes" on our experiences in our meditation. It was uncanny how often we'd receive the exact information, the same message, the same imagery.

This validation of our experiences, this sense that we're not just making it up or imagining it, was a real turning point for me. It consolidated knowledge and gave us more confidence to trust our own gut instinct, to essentially trust ourselves. We received healing tools, sacred geometry, and many messages. It was a gentle touch of encouragement to continue doing what we were doing, to continue to be of service for the Earth, people, animals, and ourselves, to honor a sense of connectedness in all things that encompass life. The importance of just "being" in and with nature was also celebrated. That day changed us; it was like we got new information coded into our DNA.

Later on that evening, we sat next to the fire and looked at the crystal-clear night sky. The stars seemed particularly bright that night and the sky was unusually active. There was a greater sense of connectedness to space. It felt like we were part of it; we could sense the movement in the stars. There didn't seem to be any time or space. We were mesmerized by the stars, the sound of the night, the water, the fire burning, almost like a newborn seeing light for the first time; the whole concept of space seemed magical. I applied some of these teachings in my life and in my sessions. I observed transformations that were undeniable.

Learnings to Share From Visions

- We are all one.
- Earth needs healing.
- When you meditate take a moment to send love into the Earth. Imagine a beam of light going down from your heart into the heart of the Earth.
- Thank the Earth for all she gives you and connect from a place of love.
- We are custodians of the Earth; we must protect her.
- Love, respect, and look after all elements of nature.
- Rocks, rivers, air, animals, and plants all have essences and healing properties.
- Tread lightly and kindly on your Mother Earth.
- Sacred geometry has frequencies and vibrations that can activate healing, protection, guidance.
- Trust your intuition; never ignore a hunch.

- Ask for guidance, quieten your mind, and listen.
- Be mesmerized by our ability to see beauty and magic in nature.

Does Your Life Represent Your Values?

Living a life that represents who you are is a wonderful practice. It allows you to feel in harmony with what you stand for. When your actions represent your values, you are clear about who you are, you can engage with the world with purpose. This creates an internal sense of well-being and synchronicity. To do this, you must first be clear about your values. Values are belief systems and principles that develop throughout your life. Your values are developed within the home environment, school, and societal influences. They play a significant role in guiding your behaviors. What are some of your important values?

Some examples are your ideas of love, equality, truth, justice, freedom. Everyone has different ideas of how beliefs are assigned value. What you value is a very personal thing and is completely subjective. What might be of value to one person might be completely irrelevant for the next. Values end up guiding your decisions and behaviors. Living a life that honors and represents what you value is beautiful. It has a tremendous impact on your happiness and well-being. By doing this, you're essentially being authentic with yourself and life.

Living an authentic life helps create harmony within you. This allows you to act in a way that represents what you believe in. It increases a sense of personal satisfaction. If you value looking after older people and see a lady struggling to cross the street, what would you do? You might be in a hurry to go somewhere and you decide to stop and help her cross the road. It may delay you a few minutes, but you feel good you acted in that kind way because you did something that was in accord with your values. When you do things that you value, it increases a sense of fulfilment and joy. It's not just about feeling good because you helped someone cross the street; it goes deeper than that. It's because you would feel disappointed in yourself if you acted in a way that was against what you think is important. This is when you start to notice that your relationship with yourself must be clear on who you are and what you stand for. When you have clarity around this, you act with clear intention. You doubt yourself less and feel sure of yourself.

Think about what you are dedicating your time to; are they things that really matter? This is a great way to notice if you are truly living an authentic life. Being genuine with yourself is key. This is incredibly beneficial for your emotional, psychological, and physical well-being. When you do this, there is a sense of being "at peace" with yourself.

How can you begin to live a life that is more conscious and awake? Start asking yourself what is really important to you. What makes you smile, what gets you feeling passionate and motivated? Look at aspects of your life and see what triggers powerful emotions within you. Look for strong emotions that spark passion. Do you have feelings of intense anger against animal cruelty, racism, or the environment? These are your guides to knowing what you're aligned to. What aspects of life do you connect to and resonate with? Allow yourself to explore these concepts a little further. Ask yourself the question, why do I get upset about animal cruelty/racism/environment? What is it about them that I don't like? Why don't I like those things? What would I change about it? Really start to dig deep and give yourself the opportunity to get to know yourself. Understand why you hold strong feelings and beliefs about things.

In this process, start to question some of the beliefs you hold. Question yourself on why you think and feel the way you do. Oftentimes, you adopt a set of values that has been passed down through generations. Families and cultures tend to have strong values, very rarely do people question them from an introspective point of view. You might not agree on arranged marriages, for example, because you married someone you love, but do you understand the "why" behind your disagreement? Why do you disagree? Is it that you believe in freedom of choice? Is it that you believe in women's rights? Is it that you simply don't want to be told what to do? Understanding why will provide you with greater insight as to who you are. You see, in a world that is bombarded with too much information, opinions on social media, and platforms for anyone to voice their beliefs, it can get confusing. You can get sucked into a vortex of voicing and liking or disliking comments, posts on social media, politicians, etc., but do you really know why?

Think about food, for example. Do you value fresh food? Most people would say YES, but why? Is it because you value the nutritional aspect of it? You want to get good value for money? You want to make sure it's organic and pesticide-free? You value the health impact it will have on you? You value that it comes from a farm that has good practices? The number of reasons is endless; knowing your why is so important.

"I think it's beautiful the way you sparkle when
you talk about the things you love"
—Atticus

Who Are You?

Get clear on who you are, do some research on what you value and notice how your body reacts to the material you're reading. Tune in to your inner moral compass. This will help you to get a good idea of what you stand for. Observe your life; start assessing what you dedicate your time to. Think about what you put into your mind, what you read, what you watch, who you follow on social media and why. What conversations do you have that you value and enjoy? What kind of people do you surround yourself with?

Start analyzing how you're spending your time and on what. If someone were to observe you, what would they see? Do your actions, behaviors, and words represent your values? Take note of how aligned you are with your own value system. If you do this and realize you're completely off and not living a life according to your values, don't despair. Gently recognize that and find ways of making slow changes. Figure out what you don't like and begin to understand why. It's important to understand why you do the things you do. This is part of living an awake conscious life. If you are to grow in your depth, you must know yourself. Ask yourself if you're actually willing to change? If the answer is no, don't beat yourself up. Just sit with it for a little bit. Get acquainted with your ideas, give yourself time. If the answer is yes, then make the time to understand why you want to change.

Sometimes, it is hard to know where to start, maybe you've held onto old values and beliefs your family handed down to you. You might think you need to continue holding onto them because they are so familiar to you or because it's expected of you. I want you to live your life on your own terms. That doesn't mean you scrap everything and disrespect others; it means you are in alignment with your own beliefs and ideas. It takes great courage to do this;

be courageous enough to honor yourself. Gratitude will be your loyal friend that will hold your hand along this journey. Figuring out what you're grateful for is a good start.

What Are You Grateful For? That Is The Question...

As mentioned in Chapter 3, gratitude provides great benefits to your life. Discovering what you are grateful for can guide you to get clear on your values. Think about the things you value in your life. What are you grateful for that maybe you take for granted? Are you grateful for your health, friends, work? Practicing gratitude trains your brain to focus on aspects of life you value. By thinking about the things you're grateful for, you begin to notice them. What you focus on you expand. So, this trains your brain to have those things you value more present.

Make a List of What You Value

- What is it about that thing/idea/person that you value?
- How much time do you spend on things you value?
- Are there any changes you need to make?
- Celebrate little wins in life (getting to work on time, sending that email, sticking to a new routine).
- Share your positive feelings with those you love; learn to express yourself lovingly.
- Engage in random acts of kindness. Give away your parking ticket, help someone carry their shopping bags.
- Call your friends and family when you know they're going through a tough time.
- Don't just think about doing something nice; do it!

- Journal things you're grateful for. Take a moment to think about it and feel it; don't just write it like a shopping list.
- Use all of your senses when describing what you are grateful for.

Make time for these activities so you can be true to yourself. I know time is precious and most people feel time deprived, but let's get creative. Think about ways you could feel less rushed every day. It might be as simple as getting up 10 minutes earlier or going to bed earlier. The simple act of not rushing will be beneficial. Make time for a good morning routine, a spiritual practice. It might be journaling, meditation, stretching, or having a quiet cup of tea before you start your day. Start to make little changes in your life that you know will have a positive impact. Starting your day calmly will set the tone for the rest of the day. When you are aligned to your values, these changes don't seem so hard. Make time to understand yourself better so you can feel that your life genuinely represents what you value.

Awesome Habits For An Awesome Day

1. Exercise first thing in the morning, even if it's jumping around or dancing to a song for a few minutes. Movement allows the blood to flow and wakes you up. It energizes your metabolic system increases endorphins and makes you feel good. Just move!
2. Do something new and difficult every day.
3. Do the hardest things first; get them out of the way. Then do the things you enjoy. This helps you start your day with a sense of accomplishment; it increases a sense of confidence, and you start to challenge yourself more.

4. Give yourself time to be still and meditate.
5. Allow your ideas to come to the surface, observe yourself from a space of quietness. There is great beauty in silence.
6. Journal, write, and get to know yourself.

Use Your Senses

Knowing what you love to hear, smell, touch, see, and taste will also give you a good idea of what you value. Your senses have an important role in activating feelings and sensations in your body. Smells also play a vital role in calming your CNS and refreshing your cognitive abilities. The olfactory system is linked to your brain and the development of memories. Smells can carry profound meaning and trigger memories easily.

Think of the smell of fresh baked cookies or bread your grandmother made. It brings back memories of love and warmth, that feeling of biting into something warm and tasty. The love poured into it is felt. If these types of memories are positive and vivid for you, think about why that might be? Is it that home-cooked food smells good and you value the effort gone into making it? When was the last time you baked cookies or made a meal from scratch that felt nourishing? Use your senses to get to know yourself; this is part of slowing down. When you hold that cup of coffee in your hands, feel the warmth; take a moment to close your eyes and smell the coffee. These tiny moments of being present connect you to your body, to the experience you're having right there and then. It allows you to be in the present moment. When you are present, you allow yourself to be open. With this open demeanor, you welcome life in and open up to having experiences. This sense of presence is grounding; it has gifts that go beyond the perception of the naked eye.

Being present allows you to value what's right in front of you. Notice daily what you love and value; it might be staring at you without you noticing it. Do you love the sound of rain on a cold winter day? Maybe you just need to sit by your window with a warm drink and watch the rain for a few minutes. If you love this, taking time out, even just 10 minutes, to watch the rain can bring you great joy. Taking this time out from your busy day allows you to feel connected. You tap in to the feeling of awe and magic in everyday moments. This creates a lovely feeling of harmony during the routine of the day.

What sounds do you resonate with? Calming and soothing sounds might be grounding at the end of the day. Create environments of sound that give you what you need. Upbeat music for motivation or binaural beats for relaxation. Maybe live music makes your heart sing but yet you don't spend much time enjoying this. Unearth what needs to change in your life to spend more time doing these things you love. Sounds have a powerful way of transporting you to other realms; use them to create the states you wish to experience more frequently.

Touch is really special; it is the most fundamental way of knowing you are safe and loved as infants. Notice if you like to hug others; if so, do you do it often enough? Observe if you feel more comfortable avoiding physical contact. If so, set clear boundaries to have that respected. Figure out what "feels" right to you. Do you like the way your bedsheets feel? This may create a sense of comfort and safety. You spend a third of your life in bed, does it feel good to be in it? Maybe you dislike your bed but don't make an effort to make it nicer. You might love the feeling of your pet's fur; do you spend enough time just petting your pet? Get in to the habit of slowing down and surrounding yourself with textures that feel good.

Look around your home and notice what you see. Are there things that represent what you love? Do you like what you see when you walk in the door? If there is clutter everywhere and it makes you feel unsettled, make some time to clear it out. Clutter creates disharmony in your mind; you will generally think better in a tidy space. Your home should be treated as your sanctuary. You are in it for long stretches of time. What you see sends messages to your brain. Surround yourself with colors and images that inspire you, objects and pictures that fill you with joy, peace, or love when you look at them. Fill your spaces with life-giving images, uplifting pictures. Create a home environment that has the energy you desire until you absolutely love what you see when you are at home.

Do you value watching a good sunset and getting lost in the colors of the changing sky? If so, how much time do you dedicate to watching the sky morph in shapes and colors? The ten minutes you take out of your busy schedule to watch the sky put on a show at sunset won't make or break your day. But it might just fill your heart with joy. That joy will have a greater impact upon you than dedicating another ten minutes to whatever you're doing. Once again, bring stillness and moments of beauty into your life. Sometimes, all you need is just to press pause and watch the sky for a few minutes to recharge.

Explore your senses, fill your environment with things that bring you joy. Make time to do things you love. This could be as simple as putting on your favorite music in the car. It could be making sure your bedroom is tidy and clearing out clutter. This might make you feel at ease and value a clean space. Everything in your internal and external environment affects the way you feel. Create spaces in your life that support your growth.

People are yearning a sense of connectedness, searching for the divinity within them. But days are filled with to-do tasks and mindless scrolling on social media. Craft time to do simple things that hold meaning. Welcome stillness and quiet solitude. By harnessing this skill to be still, you momentarily let go of the push-pull nature of busy life. Stillness allows you to feel grounded, to feel connected to a bigger picture. When you cultivate this, it becomes easier to be present and mindful of what is important to you. Sometimes, a simple ritual will settle you down. It could be arranging rocks in a shape or lighting some candles and saying a prayer. These little rituals can help you slow down, ground yourself back into your body, and only take a moment. The more you can do this throughout your day, the more easily your life will flow. Ceremonies have the power to honor the mystical; it's beautiful if you can bring this into your daily awareness. People are yearning for experiences that connect them to the divine. Design habits that connect to your own divine essence.

The more you know yourself the better you can express your needs. This will improve all your relationships.

How You Use Time Is The Key

Time is such a funny concept. Does it even exist? Our lives revolve around timeframes, alarms, numbers here and there. You are governed by it in every waking moment. You most likely bill for your time and figure out your life based on time. Time is the greatest commodity. It is your most precious resource. To have time to do the things you really value can be tricky.

I'm very aware that not everyone has a lot of time on their hands; not everyone has the luxury to meditate and have a blissful start to the day. Oftentimes, you're up and running trying to keep up with multiple commitments: things that need to be done, people who need to be fed, deadlines you need to meet. They all take up your precious time. Life often gets in the way, distracting you from what you value. This is part of real life; but there is a way.

You have more time than you think; choosing how you use it is the key. I'm going to challenge you to assess how you use your time. If you value your health but feel you don't have enough time, have a long hard think about it. How truthful are you being with yourself? There are possibly moments in your day you could be exercising, but you're distracted by other things. Are you spending time on social media or in front of the television instead of doing push ups? Could you potentially be out going for a quick jog around the block? You could even take the stairs instead of the elevator to give your heart a lift. Tiny changes can give you great results and impact your life. Be creative when you are making changes, especially if you are time deprived.

When you arrive home from work or study, you could stop in your driveway and do three minutes of deep breathing. Put on your favorite song and sing like a rock star. The more you can fill your day with little but meaningful things, the better your life will be. Simple. I want you to connect to the idea that there are small but significant changes you can implement right now. These changes will have a profound impact in the long term.

Think about the things you could do first thing in the morning that would have a significant impact on your day. A quick jog, dance, calm cup of tea, whatever rocks your boat. At midday, you can meditate on your lunch break, read pages of your book, watch the rain with a cup of hot chocolate. I encourage you to let your heart sing. Do the things you love; you don't need to make massive changes to feel the benefits. You are honoring your values; you are mindfully choosing how to spend your time. This will dictate how your life unfolds, the story you write. Realize that you are choosing in every moment; slowing down lets you be more mindful.

When you start to figure out who you are and what you value, life takes on a greater sense of purpose. Implementing these changes will make you feel more empowered and satisfied with your life choices. You'll start to honor yourself, your beliefs, and your needs. By doing this, you'll start creating a more positive relationship with yourself, this allows the internal life force you carry to shine. It will make you feel good and glow with life force; you'll become more magnetic. You're attractive when you glow; it spikes people's curiosity so they will want to know what you're doing. Start your own social experiment now; spend time on what you love and notice how the world around you responds.

If you're currently going through major life changes and challenges, these little acts won't solve your problems, not right away. If you look after yourself and use your time wisely, you can at least find things that will help you settle, activities that can support you slowing down, relaxing, even laughter. It will give your body rest and respite from the stress. Doing things that make you feel good will activate greater emotional resilience. It will strengthen your ability to deal with the challenges you face. Internal harmony will help you sleep better, unwind, connect. If that's all you get, then you're already on a good path. Be aware that every tiny little step you take in the right direction has a significant impact. It might be the powerful yet gentle act of being kind to yourself. This may provide you with insight into your own relationship and how influential that can be.

Like anything new, you will need to be patient with yourself. Figure out what you value, how to prioritize your time and start making small changes. Allow things to settle in; let these ideas and concepts just sit with you. You are learning how to get to know yourself better and train your brain. Be nice to yourself, don't expect massive changes to happen right away. Don't throw these ideas and concepts away like any other self-help book you might have tried. Be calm, be patient, be gentle, and know there is magic unfolding under the surface. Explore and see what fits, notice what has the greatest impact on your day. Play and discover who you are and what works best for you. Believe in yourself and in your ability to transform.

"Nature does not hurry,
yet everything is accomplished."
—Lao Tzu

Make Mandalas, Make Art With Nature

- Use rocks and make a circle; fill it with twigs or flowers and arrange them in a way that "feels" right to you.
- Then either sit inside it, or outside it and imagine you are creating a field of energy. Channeling all the love and healing into your body, into the Earth, or both.

CASE STUDY: Joseph Wins His Wife Back

Joseph was distraught at the thought that his wife and little daughter might leave him. He was only thirty-seven years old, and life had crumbled before his eyes. He'd been married for five years and had a two-year-old daughter. They had big dreams when they got married to build a house, form a family, and be happy.

He'd strayed from his family and had fallen into a vicious cycle of overworking, spending all his free time at the gym and drinking, and spending money on sports cars. His wife was fed up and had packed her bags ready to go. That was when I met him. Joseph was full of anger, frustration, and guilt; most of all, he was scared and sad. Like many young men, he just wanted to work as hard as he could to provide for his family. The stress of life, increasing financial pressures, overworking, alcohol, and lack of sleep had broken him. His marriage had crumbled, and he didn't understand why.

Joseph had come from a working-class family; strong work ethics were part of his upbringing; he needed to provide for his family. He remembered his father working long hours, and that's what he thought he needed to do also. The problem was that he had put himself under so much stress financially that he was no longer present in his relationship. He began to get angry at his wife and daughter; arguments would occur daily. Instead of sorting them out, he'd go to the gym for hours on end. Unfortunately, he wouldn't just go home afterwards; he'd go to the local pub and have a few drinks with his friends. This created distrust in their relationship, as his wife would call, and he wouldn't answer the phone. He felt he couldn't deal with any more stress. His beloved wife, once a priority, now seemed like a source of stress to him. He loved her but felt frustrated and irritated by her; they had disconnected. He couldn't think of a life without her and his daughter, but it was not working out.

Joseph was also beginning to feel angry all the time; he'd act out in aggressive ways at work. This was putting his livelihood at risk. He was irritable and frustrated all the time. He started making mistakes, and was putting his own safety and that of his colleagues at risk. The stress was affecting his capacity to think straight and execute the right decisions. His only source of relief was lifting heavy weights at the gym and drinking alcohol. This was creating a dependency on alcohol; and it was beginning to make him feel depressed.

During therapy, Joseph was able to align to some of his values, family values he held close to his heart he needed to remember. He also realized that maybe he was putting too much pressure on himself to live up to an expectation. He acknowledged that he was dedicating too much time to things that didn't matter at the end of the day. He wasn't giving his wife and daughter the time of day. And, although he was working hard to provide for his family, he was not present. That kind of defeats the purpose. Joseph had a good heart, but he'd gotten lost along the way. He understood he needed to take some financial pressure off and make some serious decisions. He had to find a way of reconnecting to his wife and daughter and communicate more openly.

Joseph made a financial plan; he'd sell two of his sports cars (he owed money on) and would consider downsizing to a smaller house. He realized it was useless to work so hard if he couldn't spend time with his family and on his hobbies. He didn't need that added stress. He also began counseling with his wife to address their communication issues and solve the marital problems they were facing.

In hypnosis, Joseph was able to significantly reduce his level of stress. He was able to stop the worrying and negative thinking causing anxiety and stress. He released the negative association he'd created in his mind of his wife being a source of stress. He connected to his emotions and feelings and aligned to his values. He let go of guilt and shame for not being who he thought he needed to be. He let go of the ever-present fear he felt that was activating his survival mechanism, making him on edge and defensive all the time. He arrived at a much calmer space; he began to apply the self-hypnosis techniques I taught him to help him sleep better and calm down.

He began to feel more in control of his life. From this space, he was able to think clearer, perform better at work, and get in touch with his feelings. He was no longer trying to escape his stress with endless hours at the gym lifting heavy weights and drinking until he couldn't remember who he was. He found a better balance, still physically active but with a different intention, the energy wasn't so aggressive and competitive. He'd sometimes swap his gym sessions for a run at the beach or his local park. Sometimes, he'd involve his wife and daughter, and they would take a ball and run around in the playground. He found a way of combining what was important to him (family and fitness).

Joseph and his wife began to communicate better. Their marriage and sense of connection improved immediately. He was more present, more relaxed, and more considerate of his family's needs. He was out of survival mode; this allowed him be more aware of everyone around him. He found his spark and began to feel happier, more relaxed, and light-hearted. They ended up selling their house, renting for a few years to save some money, and bought a smaller house with a smaller mortgage closer to his parents. He felt free of social pressures and more confident to be himself. He had learned good coping mechanisms, started meditating daily, and used his self-hypnosis regularly. He felt more joy than he had in years. He felt at ease, more love for himself and his wife, and it was showing in every aspect of his life. He saved his marriage and created a new life; he built strong emotional resilience and was more aware of who he was and how to face challenges positively.

"Don't be a prisoner of your comfort zone;
it will keep you in a mediocre life"
—Kali

Exercises

- Learn to listen to your body.
- Allow yourself time to feel the emotions that come up.
- Surround yourself with people who will support this process for you and with you.
- Give yourself time to discover who you really are and what inspires you.
- Write down what you value, why you value it, and how your actions could change to represent your values more clearly.
- Feel a sense of inner peace and tranquillity with your decisions.
- Figure out what feels good in your body.
- Write this statement down and say it out loud:
  - "I'm filled with love, joy, and vitality; I allow creative ideas to flow through me easily and I am happy and at peace with myself!"

My feet walked along the beautiful coast.
The wet sand held my steps.
She saluted me with her roaring waves,
I stood in her water with open arms,
I let her hold me as I poured my heart out.
I sent mother nature my tears of fears,
I sent her my love and gratitude for her beauty
and healing.
I let her soft sand dunes hold me,
I sat and watched the waves rolling in,
I heard songs of the birds whisper hope in my ears,
I surrendered and let the breeze blow my
sadness away.

Kalí

CHAPTER 7

DARKNESS ALLOWS YOUR LIGHT TO SHINE

Spirit Takes The Breath Away, Chile, 2017

I placed crystals on her heart; I held her hand and sat beside her bed. Her hand felt warm and soft, I sensed love pouring from my heart into hers. The beeping sounds from the machines in the ICU room felt loud and irritating. There was a stillness, a solemn moment that was hanging in time. I repeated "I love you" in my mind and felt her response in my heart. She took her last breath and off she went into the next realm. Some moments stay with you forever; this was one of them. My mother had died in my hands. In this sacred moment of transition, it was an honor to hold the woman who first held me. She held me as I took my first breath, and I held her as she took her last breath. There was something so beautiful in this closing of a cycle. It was a birth that I could hold and support this time, birthing my mother into the Spirit realm.

I felt privileged that she felt safe enough for us to hold her as she departed from her body. How beautiful to be held by your loving family in that very moment of transition. It struck me to feel peace and beauty while my heart broke as I witnessed her physical departure.

The days prior to her death, my brother, father, and I had turned the cold ICU room into a space of love and healing. We hung crystals and Jewish prayers on her IV stand, we made essential oil sprays to freshen her up and played her favorite music. We'd massage her scalp and her feet and sat on her bed recalling funny stories and telling her we loved her. We made sure to always let her know that if she needed to rest or let go, to do so. None of us expected my mother to die, she had been well for years and hadn't shown any signs of illness. Ten days prior to her death, she woke up disoriented. We got on a plane and flew to her immediately. You never know when your time is up. You never know if the next time you say goodbye to someone will be the last time you see them.

Six months prior to this had been the first time I had truly experienced a loving and steady relationship with my mother. We had an entire month of adoring each other, traveling the world and creating a beautiful bond. We had finally healed our relationship. It had blossomed and we felt comfortable and joyful with each other. Little did I know that would be the last and only time that would occur. Although it was short lived, it was the most wonderful gift life could give.

The wonderful thing is that our loving connection didn't stop after she died. Time passed, and I felt the loss, the grief, the pain; I had to learn how to live without her. In this learning, I created a new relationship with her. I'd "feel" her presence, and, in so doing, I began a journey that would make our love grow. I felt she was present but free. I started to honor her life, speak to her at her favorite beach spots, and say good night to her as I drifted off to sleep. I'd visit the ocean and let the sea breeze blow my tears away when I missed her. I wrote her letters, sharing my life and read them to her under the moonshine. I surrounded myself with people who supported me, who could hold space for me in this time of grief.

I didn't quite understand how but I felt my love for her grew. It was one of the hardest experiences in my life; it is also one of the ones that has taught me the most. So, in honoring the memory of my beloved mother, I thank her for her death. Her death has enlightened me in many areas of my life; it has revealed some of the most mystical aspects of existence. When you can look at life like that, everything is a gift, even if it hurts.

In Darkness I Shall Shine

Life is full of ups and downs; it has tragedies, heartbreaks, and suffering. Knowing how to navigate these feelings is a crucial aspect of having an empowered mind. Knowing that you can experience all the emotions that life throws at you without crumbling is a powerful skill. Feeling fully without losing view of the bigger picture is resilience.

Ancient cultures around the world have rituals that delve into the mysterious. Potions are drunk, mushrooms picked, and trancelike states take over the bodies of countless people in a search for the divine. Humans are curious about what is on "the other side," the death of the ego, what happens to the soul, heaven, and hell. All these concepts explore the ideas of life and who you are. Being able to understand and hold all of life's experiences as just that, experiences, can alleviate the suffering caused by holding onto the human body.

You are in constant transformation; your body sheds cells every day, your mind is constantly expanding and evolving. In some sense, transformation is part of your daily life. The biggest transformation everyone will face is death. When a spirit decides to leave the body, it transforms. The body morphs and goes back into the Earth. These mutations are observed every day; the sky change colors as daytime turns into nighttime. But, somehow, the finality of death's transformation creates great suffering and mystery. It could very well be that the attachment to the physical body is causing suffering more than death itself.

Knowing how to navigate these states of suffering is really significant to your well-being. Being surrounded by people who support you, engaging in activities that nourish you, and taking good self-care are paramount. Allowing yourself healthy ways of processing difficult emotions is key. Breathe them out, sing them out, walk them off. Find ways of allowing yourself to feel, to cry, to be vulnerable. This is a time to show compassion to yourself, to others, and to those nasty little voices that fill minds with fear. In this process, a cup of tea can feel nourishing. Sitting down on the ground creating intricate shapes with sticks and stones can be soothing. When you face life's challenges, bring in all the great coping mechanisms by your side. This is a time to express your feelings and needs and let people and life in to support you. Let yourself be embraced by nature. Nature heals; all ancient traditions know this.

A caterpillar, cocooned in its "gooping" process, lets go of what it was to become something else, a butterfly. I'm sure the caterpillar has no idea that the transformation it is undergoing will result in a beautiful metamorphosis. Similarly, a baby being born, while in the safe space of the warm womb, has all its needs met. That's all it's ever known, warmth and safety. During the birthing process, suddenly, there is stress, heart rate increases, contractions take place, and the serenity of this tranquil haven is disrupted. Everything is disturbed, little does the baby know it will come to a new beginning. The baby might feel like it is actually dying. Once the baby is born and has gone through that transformative experience of birth, it will awaken. It will see colors it cannot even imagine, sense touch from its mother, and hear sounds that are as clear as day. Essentially, the newborn has experienced the death of its prenatal life so far as it was aware.

Only in death can we truly appreciate how delicate our existence is. Death is something everyone will encounter, whether it's the death of a loved one, a pet, someone you know, or simply your own. Yet it is one of the hardest experiences you will go through, one of the most unspoken aspects of life. Society doesn't really teach you how to deal with it or prepare yourself for it. The unspoken truth creates fear; it breeds uneasiness and confusion. The more you can embrace this as an aspect of life, the better you will be able to step into it. Death happens in many forms; it can be the end of a relationship, the close of an era, or the dissolution of your ego. The important aspect of this is the ever-changing nature of existence.

"Even a happy life cannot be without a measure of darkness,
and the word happy would lose its meaning if it were not
balanced by sadness. It is far better to take things as
they come along with patience and equanimity"
—Carl Jung

Magical Rituals Can Heal

Rituals are a beautiful way of allowing emotions to be expressed through your heart. It could be the simple placing of flowers together in a shape and giving thanks for nature. It could be symbolically burning a letter expressing your negative emotions and watching the smoke take it away. Rituals transform experiences; they are the alchemy of emotions, supporting healing to unfold. A burial or spiritual ceremony is an honoring of a life. Many cultures around the world have rituals for important life events that allow meaning to be given to these experiences.

In their busy lives, people have forgotten the importance of daily rituals. They rush here, there, and everywhere. Only on major religious holy days, social pressures remind the masses to participate in rituals such as decorating a Christmas tree or writing a love letter on Valentine's day. Why only celebrate life and love a few times each year? I want you to give greater purpose and meaning to your life daily. If not daily then at least regularly. This reminds you of the delicate nature of life, to not take anything for granted, and to celebrate everything. A simple ritual that is filled with great intentions and powerful feelings can be an uncomplicated gesture. It may be lighting a candle and giving thanks for your day. A ritual allows you to align with your intent; it is expressed through your action. Practice nonattachment to an outcome at the end of your ritual and let it go. You let it go, trusting life will take care of it. Rituals give value to your life. They make the mundane seem that little bit more magical.

Create something of your own. Incorporate novel ways of engaging with yourself; let yourself explore and find out what feels right. It might be to collect shells on a beach walk and make a shape with them on the sand. It could be placing a flower on top of your pile of work and "blessing" it with abundance.

Involve your loved ones in this so you can teach others and engage in a different way. Something unspoken occurs in the sharing of sacred rituals that bonds people. This experience heals beyond what the eye can see; it is a language of the heart. The more you can embody this ability to express the language of the heart, the greater your healing will be. Stepping out of your mind and into your heart can generate great power. Take conscious steps to feel connected to the power that lies within you and make a life worth living.

Imagine gathering rocks or crystals to make a circle. You align with your intention; it might be to create abundance in your day. You sit with someone you value. As you place each rock or item into the circle give it a feeling or meaning: "joy," "laughter," "wealth," "opportunities," and say the word as you place the rock in the circle. The other person does the same thing. When you finish, you have created a shape that holds all these emotions. You may say out loud or silently in your mind, "I give thanks for this beautiful day filled with joy, laughter, wealth, and abundant opportunities." You may want to close your eyes and just repeat those words or sit silently. Feel the emotions and your intention. This is a beautiful activity to do that you can easily incorporate into your life.

Write inspiring words on a piece of paper, decorate them, put them in a bowl, and make a lucky dip. Pick one out blindly and see what shows up for you that day. Let's say you pick confidence. Ask yourself how you can embody confidence on this day. These are light-hearted, simple, yet powerful activities you can blend into your days. It can also be a fun way of teaching children to create their days with intention. By doing this, you are aligning your intention with emotion and action. All aspects of creation come into play here. You can make these exercises as elaborate or as simple as you'd like. Get creative with them and just give it a go.

You needn't be religious or spiritual to engage in these activities. The purpose here is to give your life greater meaning, to activate your brain's neural pathways with intent, to take a moment of calmness and stillness to play and bring the divine aspects of existence into your daily life. This provides a sense of expression, creativity, emotion regulation, and a little bit of magic. Life is about magic; magical moments are unfolding everywhere on any given day. Create your own magic, knowing it can heal. How wonderful is that? You have the power to do that.

This whole book is about how to heal, how to connect, and how to shine. It's about how you can do that with your loved ones in life and after death has taken away a loved one. Death allows you an opportunity to review your life, review the life you had with that loved one. Sometimes, it also provides you with the opportunity to reassess what you value and if anything needs to change in your own life. Death can be a real teacher and guide if you let it be. It can transform you and give you permission to create yourself anew.

Although it is important to allow death to be a teacher, don't wait for death to knock on your door to make changes in your life. People often wait for tragedies or broken bones to take good care of themselves and their relationships. Make it a life choice to look after and cherish everything you have right now. Don't live a life filled with regrets; don't wait for the perfect moment. Be courageous; act now while the ones you love are still around. I'm the first to admit that life can be challenging, outright distressing, and painful at times. So, I'm saying this from a place of love, knowing how hard it can be at times. Dedicating time to heal your own wounds and go through your own process of growth is beneficial before you heal other relationships.

The Medicine Of The Andes. Animals Guide The Way

Nature holds healing qualities in its plants, elements, and animal world. Native cultures from around the world have engaged in the healing and mystical aspects using nature's gifts. Medicine men and women have played an important role, healing communities since antiquity. They are referred to by many names; I shall simply use the word shaman. Mystical shamans nurture a sacred and symbolic relationship with Mother Earth. Modern cultures around the world are obsessed with lotions and potions that promise eternal youth and the hope of magical states. People around the globe search for rejuvenating creams, painkilling substances, and stimulating beverages. People are in a constant relationship with nature, seeking its healing properties. Just look at all the coffee drinkers around the world, stimulating their minds with this magical elixir. Some of these gifts from nature provide access to other worlds, trancelike states, and spiritual experiences. The search for altered states of consciousness and the journey into the divine magnetically draws people from all walks of life. Shamans use their mystical qualities to explore the healing characteristics of plants, energy, and the spirit world. Shamans are a bridge from the physical to the spiritual world, communicating with the spiritual aspects of all life.

Whether you believe in such things or not, some kind of medicine magic has been part of human existence since the beginning of time, a link between life and death, reality and mysticism. A shaman is there to heal, to protect the community, to be one with nature, and guide the way. A shaman is an earth keeper, a seer, a speaker of truth and transformation. Energy medicine, musical instruments, and plants are common objects used in the healing process. The sound of a deep drum can take a person into another state; the careful preparation of potions can propel you into other realms. In essence, it's no secret that nature holds the blueprint to healing.

Sometimes, in modern life, you can drift away from your connection to everything. You stray from your connection to yourself, nature, and the ethereal. Life can sometimes seem too dense, too stuck in the 3D reality. Shamanism gives a perspective that allows you to think of life in a bigger way. It allows you to go into the archetypal realm of the symbolic and mysterious. Great imagination and creativity accompany this. By incorporating greater awareness and imagination, you can expand your mind. This often allows you to see the bigger picture and remind yourself of grander things in life. This can be a source of inspiration in moments of greatness and a true blessing in challenging times.

Now, before you think about skipping this bit, as it may seem a little "woo woo," allow yourself to explore these ideas. I am by no means an expert in the field; I humbly aim to share my understanding from the teachings I have received. In energy medicine of the people of the Andes, certain animals and coordinates represent specific aspects of life. I share these with you so you can embody some of these aspects in your own journey of empowerment. I will share some of the qualities the animals represent. The animals that hold spiritual qualities in this tradition are hummingbird, eagle, serpent, and jaguar.

The north is represented by the hummingbird. The hummingbird represents being able to move in all four directions. Hummingbird acts with faith. She fills her body with life's sweetest nectar. She takes off on her migratory journey from North America to South America. Hummingbird has faith as she travels across the continent with no guarantee of when the next feed is; she just goes. Hummingbird only drinks from life's sweetest nectar, she fills her body with this elixir that will fuel her flight for kilometers on end.

Hummingbird is the teller of truth; she sees through situations with pure clear vision.

The east is represented by the eagle. The eagle embodies Christ consciousness, a consciousness of oneness, unity. The eagle has the ability to rise above any situation and see the big picture from a bird's eye view. The eagle soars high in the skies with great strength and agility, always having his eye on his prey while flying above with a view and perspective of the whole landscape. The eagle can see the unlimited vision of life from the heights of the heavens.

The south is represented by serpent. The serpent embodies all the magic of being in the body, with her belly up against the ground. She is connected to the earth, grounded, connected in this way to Pachamama. She has the courage to shed old skin and let go of what no longer serves her. She has faith she will grow the new skin she needs. Grounded and connected to her body, she embodies knowledge and sexuality.

The west is represented by jaguar. The jaguar embodies the ability to be a night warrior, bringing his night vision or light into the darkness. Jaguar is always transforming, camouflaging, and moving with confident grace. Always focused on his goal, his prey, moving his body boldly. He walks through the jungle with an unshakeable presence. He carries his magic by knowing he does not need light to illuminate his way. He brings light to the situation and makes himself comfortable in the darkness.

Embodying Secrets Of Nature

By outlining the qualities and symbolic meaning of animals and nature, you can use them to understand yourself better. Nature is your faithful teacher. Imagine how you can embody and embrace different aspects of these spirit animals into your own lives.

Hummingbird is tiny yet so powerful. How can you begin to drink from life's sweetest nectar? What could this mean in real life? Imagine deciding to spend time with the people and friends that encourage, love, and support you. The quality of your life would dramatically change if you did this instead of wasting time on people who criticize you. Can you start having more encouraging and empowering thoughts and feelings? Can you have the faith to go forth, knowing you have what you need to get you through the journey from A to B. Make important decisions in your life, having faith in yourself. Act with faith, see the truth you hold within you, and make bold decisions with clarity.

Eagle medicine encourages you to rise above your current situation. Think about how many situations you are stuck in that you could rise above. Let go of the little things you get stressed about, the arguments you dwell on, the grudges you keep. Rise above and look at the higher perspective you could embody in this situation. The other beautiful aspect of Eagle medicine is its ability to connect to Christ consciousness, oneness, the ability to feel that you are connected, that we are all one and there is no separation between things. When you rise above a situation and allow yourself to do what "love" would do, you embody oneness consciousness. When you do what's best for another or a particular situation, you ultimately do the best for yourself and the greater good. Notice how you can let go of being "stuck" in situations that may harm you like arguments or holding grudges. Interlace the principles of healing, rise above, see the bigger picture, connect to everything.

The serpent is embodied, comfortable in her own skin, so much so that it's willing to shed it. She represents the ability to be fully embodied, grounded, and present in your body, holding wisdom in your skin, held by the Earth, connected to the ground, allowing Pachamama to literally hold you as you lay your belly on her. Pay respect and attention to your body, look after your body, nourish your body. Connect to your body from a space of care and love. Let go of the "old skin" you no longer need. Shed ideas and beliefs you grew up with that no longer resonate with who you are. Let go, move on, and trust that you will grow a better skin. Love your body; it's the only one you've got. Serpent is grounded to the Earth. Walk on wet sand at the beach, walk on the earth in a forest, allow yourself to feel the ground beneath you.

Jaguar medicine can navigate darkness with grace and strength. Walk like you mean it with confident grace and strength in your step. Know that you can face the dark night of the soul with your vision. Allow yourself to feel there is magic in the darkness you're experiencing, knowing that nothing is permanent. Keep your eye on your goal like the jaguar hunts his prey, focused and determined to achieve it, committed to overcoming your fears and being your best. Knowing every single step you're taking is part of the process; it's not separate from the goal but part of it. Being present, accept where you are while making changes to move toward your goals.

Call forth the essence of animal spirits to heal, guide, and empower you. Be more discerning and choose to drink from life's sweetest nectar. Rise above challenges and see the bigger picture. Honor and connect to your body lovingly, firmly grounded on the Earth. Be the light in moments of darkness.

Embodying The Essence Of a Tree

- Stand strong with your head held high, like a tall tree.
- Make strong roots that are wide and deep; let this connect you to others who support you.
- Grow your branches strong and wide.
- Let your leaves fall when the autumn arrives.

- Hold on tightly, gathering strength from your nearby companions under the Earth when storms hit you hard.
- Share your fruits easily and generously with those who visit you.
- Provide shade, shelter, and comfort to all who pass you by.
- Give air and life force to everything around you.
- Be strong like a tree.
- Know that every season has its beauty, know that every branch that snaps off gives way to another that will take its place.
- Let go of your old skin as bark falls off.
- Give of yourself, your love, your abundance generously as you blossom with fruits hanging off you.
- Know you are always supported by an invisible source of connectedness in your roots deeply held by the Earth.
- Know you have a place in this world.
- You are valuable; you provide life force through your beaming heart.

CASE STUDY: *Carolina Shines Again*

Carolina, a woman in her fifties, initially came to see me to help her with a phobia she developed of not being able to open her mail. This was becoming problematic, as she now had a pile of unopened mail that was getting bigger than what she could handle. Her story was one of true heartbreak. She had lost her adult son a few years back in a drowning accident. Her son had swum out to help his friend who had gotten stuck in a riptide in the ocean. Neither of them came back. As any mother losing her child, Carolina was absolutely heartbroken. Her pain was palpable and paralyzing her in ways that were beginning to limit her life. She'd developed this phobia as a result of getting letters from authorities pertaining to her son's death and investigations. Despite her grief, she held herself well and navigated through life elegantly. She faced her challenges in a positive manner, but this event had shaken her to the core, and she was unable to overcome it on her own.

We explored her grief, peeling away the layers of mourning, the pain that was ever present. She understood that holding onto this pain was crippling her. Carolina had a genuinely lively bubbly spirit; she actively cared for others and generously gave of her time. She had felt disappointed, hurt, and let down amidst her grief. It is difficult to understand how grief unfolds for people; it is not a straight line or set of rules. It doesn't just go away after a year of mourning, and you don't just "get over it" either. So, as is often the case, other people carry on with their lives; they move on. The person holding the grief can feel quite lonely and isolated and, sometimes, even insulted that others have moved on. Carolina was a woman who felt she had so much to give, but she'd often feel disappointed. She didn't feel that life, friends, and family gave back in a way she expected and this was a source of hurt she carried. It was a deep yearning to love and be loved.

In our sessions, there would be glimpses of her spirit shining through in little cheeky comments. It was as if she'd open up for a second and let herself shine. This was amidst tears and the ever-present pain. Grief wasn't going anywhere; it was very real for her. She realized that grief was making her mind focus on survival and fear. She understood that she needed to befriend grief, accept her life circumstances. She was one of those patients who took most of the things we discussed on board, did her work, faced her fears, and followed through. She took full responsibility for her actions. Carolina came to the understanding that grief had seeped into all aspects of her life. This awareness brought out her determination to let it go, shed her skin. The warrior spirit rose to the surface; she was not going to let fear dictate her life any longer.

In hypnosis, Carolina was able to release the phobia, anxiety, and fear. This allowed her to step out of survival and make some room for further progress. The aim was to significantly reduce the symptoms that were having detrimental impacts on her. Grief was another layer that was deeper, it needed some time. I witnessed her transformations with reverence. The storms of grief, hurt, betrayal, and pain slowly and magically turn into valleys of hope, excitement, and love. Carolina started to transform, to blossom; she got in touch with her vitality and life force. She had found a sweet balance in feeling, accepting, and letting go. She let go of the judgments and expectations she'd had of life, accepting that life had unfolded as it did. She stepped away from her emotionally very fragile identity, scarred by grief and disappointment, and toward a strong courageous woman who faced life gracefully.

She had an idea of who she wanted to be, what her values were, and she created this ideal self in hypnosis. We worked together at shedding the layers of negativity and fear and created empowered thought patterns. Carolina built a strong sense of self, powerful emotional resilience, and unconditional self-love. She began to shine regardless of how life would unfold. She began to attract more meaningful friendships and felt more valued, appreciated, and validated. All the relationships she valued started to heal and blossom. Carolina found a way to go beyond herself. She found a way to overcome who she thought she needed to be to everyone else and simply allowed herself to just be who she was. She was unapologetically radiant, present, committed to a life of love and genuine joy. The wonderful thing was that when she let go of her attachment to getting all the things she desired, she let them in.

That was the moment life gave them to her. That's the beauty of how this magical thing we call life unfolds, when we let go, we receive.

"Your children are not your children.
They are the sons and daughters of Life's longing for itself.
They come through you but not from you,
And though they are with you yet they belong not to you."
—Khalil Gibran

Exercise

- Write a letter to your mother and your father.
- Thank them for all they have done.
- If you've had a difficult relationship with them, simply thank them for bringing you into this world.
- Tell them all the things you wish to say you have never said to them: the good, the bad, the ugly.
- Forgive them for the mistakes they have made; they too were children once, and no one teaches you how to be a parent. Understand they did their very best; that may have been giving you up. Regardless, when you forgive, some of the hurt is released.
- Now forgive yourself for holding onto any grudges you may have toward them.
- Finish the letter off with the following sentence if it feels right to you: "I thank you for bringing me into the world. I forgive you for all the hurt and pain experienced. I send you love, and I let you go free."
- Now in a safe place burn the letter and let it be taken into the sky.

As I woke to the chirping of the birds outside my window,
I had remnants of the magical night I was emerging from.
Visited by celestial beings under the radiance of the full
moon's beaming shine, they rode down the rays of
luminescent mystical light, with their celestial trumpets,
gently hovering around serenading my sleeping soul.
They whispered dreams in my ears and showered me with
inspirational sprinklings of ideas and visions of greatness.
They had heard my prayers around the fire under the
moonshine and they delivered their magic with mystical
grace.

Kalí

CHAPTER 8

GOING BEYOND BLISS

Transcendental Healing, Beulah Colorado, 2015

I looked out my window and saw a deer peering straight at me, I walked to the other side of the room and looked out another window and saw more deer. The house was surrounded by deer. In the distance, I could see deer jumping in the fields and walking down the street. This was not some strange dream; I had woken up in deer country. I was in Beulah, Colorado. I had flown across the world to dive into my subconscious on a retreat. I quickly got ready, eagerly awaiting my meeting with Jack. Jack Stucki is a scientist, music therapist, shaman, and I was about to meet him. I was so excited that I sat on the steps waiting for his arrival. I was intrigued by his knowledge and experience in the fields of integrative medicine and paranormal.

Jack arrived and he was beaming with love, almost like a white light, surrounding his body. We drove through a magnificent forest;

deer were everywhere, and I was mesmerized. The vegetation seemed magical; the greens were luminescent and the scent of the pines stimulated your senses. The trees were ancient, strong, and imposing; their leaves shimmered in the light. The air was crisp and clean and full of birds everywhere; it really was enchanting. Jack's studio and home is nestled in the heart of the mountain. On our way there, we needed to head into the heart of the canyon. I jumped out of the car to open the gate at the river crossing, leading us into the mountain reserve. You could feel the energy of the mountain, the water rushing by underneath the wooden bridge; the place felt alive. Birdsongs, water, and the leaves of the trees rattling against one another was all you could hear. I felt a real sense of adventure. Plus, we were in bear country, so there was always the anticipation of seeing a bear if we were lucky.

We traveled bordering the river with the mountain's face right up against the car along a narrow ridge. It was lush with vegetation and pleasing to the eye. We drove quite a way into the canyon and then up a steep driveway to Jack's house. Facing the river was a magnificent medicine wheel filled with the most amazing rocks, crystals, stones and sculptures. Jack had gathered these rocks and sculptures from all over the world. We arrived at the top of his driveway and were greeted by his lovely wife Judy and dog Emy Lou. I felt an overwhelming sense of love and peace there; it was so intense it literally moved me to tears within minutes of stepping out of the car.

We sat on the porch having lunch looking down toward the medicine wheel, the river, and over the mountain. It was a splendid view. Tiny hummingbirds buzzing beside us in the sunlight. A bird feeder had attracted numerous hummingbirds that were within arm's length. It was mesmerizing to go up and see them close by feeding and moving at such high speeds. Their colorful bodies changing color as the sun hit them. After lunch, we wandered down into the medicine wheel and had a look at the stones, crystals and sculptures. We took time to just sit there and absorb the atmosphere, the air was fresh. It was a cold in the shade, warm in the sun kind of day. There was a real sweetness about this place. You could literally feel the energy inside the medicine wheel. Jack had gone to a lot of effort setting up the stones in the right coordinates and creating an energetic vortex within the medicine wheel. It was palpable and beautiful. After all this getting acquainted with Jack's home and his work, we got into his studio to do some healing work.

Jack had designed several apparatuses that he used for his work. I was intrigued to see how he'd woven so many healing elements together. He had a chair that you sat in with headphones and it moved at the frequency of the sounds emitted. Then there was the "piece de resistance." A healing bed made of steel mechanically designed to move as if you were inside the womb. Several elements made this a magnificent piece of work. You lie on the bed and get hooked up to electrodes on your forehead with biofeedback tracking your brain waves. Then there are Vogel crystals hanging above your body from head to toe. Light is beamed through each crystal into your chakras. Once I was in and hooked up, I was ready to go (felt like I was about to be shot up to the moon).

I closed my eyes and tuned in to the music, shamanic drums and didgeridoo gently accompanied me into a trance state. The bed started moving in an upwards motion in unison with the music.

Through my closed eyelids I could sense the beams of colored light shooting through the crystals above me. I had no expectations, no knowledge of what would unfold; I just trusted in the experience. What was to happen literally changed the course of my life. It changed my brain and challenged my belief systems. The sounds began to get more intense, the beat of the music faster.

I allowed myself to relax into the movement of the bed and the flickering lights. I remember that moment I let myself go; I felt like I completely lost all concept of time and space. I felt I was in a dream and I started to have these images flashing through me. The visions got more intense and clearer, as if someone were showing me scenes of a movie, jumping from one scene to the next. Some scenes passed by quickly; others seemed to last forever in slow motion.

I remember distinctly having a vision of being an African man, tall and otherworldly. I felt as if I were there. I could see clearly and feel as if things were actually unfolding. In my vision I was running through a jungle effortlessly, weightless. I felt telepathically connected to the animals around me, animals running alongside me, birds flying next to me. As I felt myself running through the jungle and riverbeds, I felt in unison with the animals. We all became one mind; I could feel the beat of the drumming music moving me in unison with everything. Then the river came to an end and turned into a waterfall, my body took one big leap into the abyss, and I transformed into water and mist. I was suspended in time having the experience of being misty water. This seemed to be in slow motion, experiencing being a particle, a drop. Suddenly I was in another vision, a Native American girl by the side of a lake with a long plait and traditional dress. I stayed there for some time; the music had slowed down and so had the vision. I looked up to the sky, and, in a second, I transformed into stardust. It was all expansive; I was so many things at the same time.

All of this was happening so quickly that I had no room or time for my thoughts to doubt it, analyze it, or understand it; it just was. Then I focused my awareness from the stardust to the Earth and dived down. I found myself being the awareness of the red dirt soil of Uluru, Australia, and I was the warm earth. It was like whatever I looked at for a split second, I would then be there. This went on for a while, the visions would merge from one experience to another. My brain flooded with images, experiences, and sensations that went beyond my understanding. It was one of the most profound experiences I have ever had. I came out of this feeling exhilarated. I felt a rush of energy, a sense of love, an expansion of consciousness. I had experienced a feeling of connectedness and oneness with all. I had no concept of me as me, my body, my name, my gender; I just was. It was so bizarre, that I couldn't explain it with words or concepts that made sense. The actual sensation, having the visions was a truly blissful experience.

This experience allowed me to connect to a feeling of elation. I had been going through a challenging phase of my life and I was feeling a bit disenchanted and heavy. This experience jolted me out of that state and gave me a dose of concentrated bliss. It allowed my mind to expand and my awareness of myself evolved. My brain had been altered by this experience; it secreted chemicals that created a feeling of bliss. My brainwaves, tracked by the biofeedback machine, showed deep theta levels. The combination of the sounds, the movement, the crystals, and my openness created healing. All of this was accomplished with the powers of my mind and the healing elements Jack had created; no external substances were involved.

This experience supported my healing, it snapped me out of a space shrouded in darkness. It stimulated my brain with new possibilities and unlimited potentials. It gave me an experiential understanding of who I was (unlimited source energy). It brought to the forefront the unfathomable immensity of life. I felt I had experienced unlimited consciousness full of possibilities. This sparked an excitability within me that had lain dormant under layers of stress. Life had temporarily pulled me back into old patterns that focused on my limitations, fears, and stress. Now that had been shaken off, sung away. I felt whole once again; I went home to ME, and that changed the way I viewed and related to my life in wonderful ways. This experience was transcendental; it sped up my growth and reminded me of the magic of life once again.

Bliss Buzz—The Neurobiology Of Bliss

Altered states of consciousness can often lead to a sensation of bliss. These sublime states guide you toward openness, expansion, timelessness, and feeling radiant. Intentional calming of the mind or focusing on a sound can open the door to blissful experiences. Blissful experiences can last for hours after the experience has passed. When practiced often enough, it is even possible to experience these wonderful states in your everyday life. These blissful states of awareness stimulate the pleasure center in your brain, the nucleus accumbens. This mysterious part of the brain produces chemicals associated with feelings of euphoria, joy, and elation. It produces a sensation of trust and allows you to bond. Dopamine is one of the neurochemicals responsible for this. Dopamine is a neurotransmitter that produces feelings leading to positive mood.

Dopamine is also stimulated by external stimuli, including food, drugs, and sex. This is the high so many drug addicts chase. Trouble is, with external stimuli like drugs, the body needs more and more to get the same high. Tolerance is formed and it is no longer novel after the first time. Similar to watching a movie for the second or third time, the novelty has worn off, so it doesn't produce such a powerful reaction. In contrast, when dopamine is stimulated internally in meditation, it seems that the more you practice it, the better it gets. Some studies have examined the dopamine levels in the brains of people who are experienced in meditation (Esch, 2013). They found that an increase of 65% of dopamine was present in experienced meditators compared to nonmeditators. This is pretty amazing; you can train your brain to create states of ecstasy, bliss, exuberance.

Several altered states of consciousness and spiritual practices can have similar effects. Hypnosis, breathwork, meditation, sounds, and dance can induce similar states of elation. All of these practices allow you to experience a greater sense of who you are. Engaging with yourself in this way strengthens your self-perception. The experience of who you are becomes more pleasant and enjoyable. This will motivate you to spend more time going within. Finding ways of connecting to yourself that stimulates these feelings is powerful. You can create a way of getting to know yourself that forms an empowered sense of self.

These practices improve the functioning of your brain. When you practice meditation, for example, your brain goes into greater synchronization. Your brain's activity begins to work in a way that is harmonious; this has many benefits. Studies have shown that regular meditation allows people to deal with daily stressors more positively (Bauer, 2019). It increases emotional resilience, cognitive capacities, and a sense of control. With a calm mind and healthy brain, you allow the symphony of cognitive functions to unfold more easily. Your ability to solve problems improves, you feel more creative, and you face challenges comfortably. Sometimes, it can be as simple as listening to a particular sound like a drum or chants and let the music heal. Synchronizing to a sound like repetitive drumming stimulates the brain. It can often activate strong imagery, a loss of perception of time, and harmony in the body (Vaitl et al., 2005). The drumming sound can stimulate a sensation of becoming one with the rhythm. This increases your theta brain waves and calms the body.

Using several approaches to create changes in your brain and body can open the door to enter altered states of consciousness.

Ancient traditions have used sounds, dance, and breathing to enter trance states. Relaxation techniques also play a significant role. The combination of relaxation, breathing, and imagery creates powerful changes. The combination of these activities stimulates the brain, reducing cortisol and changing brainwaves. This allows you to float between wakeful awareness and deep relaxation, altering your state of consciousness. In hypnosis, this can be done to create a safe sensation, a positive connection to your body and your senses. A wonderful sense of relaxation overcomes you as you let go and expand your mind. This allows you to be completely immersed in your experience. Approach all aspects of this with open curiosity, with the intention of expanding your mind. Make time in your life to explore these more expansive states of being. See what lies beneath the surface of your subconscious and explore your mind. You might be pleasantly surprised to have experiences that go beyond your expectation.

Going Beyond Yourself

Bliss, transcendence, and mystical experiences are states that humans are fortunate to experience. Let's look at what is necessary to be able to even entertain the idea of having these experiences in an intentional way. First of all, if you look at Maslow's hierarchy of needs, self-transcendence is right at the top.

One of the very important aspects of self-transcendence is your ability to go beyond yourself, a sense of connectedness to a greater reality. The ability to tap in to states that feel like you're floating on a cloud of awe are more likely to happen on a regular and intentional basis if you feel you've achieved self-actualization. When you've met your needs and have moved toward your goals, you create more space in your mind for experiences of wonder.

You may have transcendental experiences like I did with Jack, in a beautiful setting with an exceptional healer; but wouldn't it be wonderful to master the ability to intentionally create these states? It's like you get a glimpse of the magic of life and this allows you to see life from a different perspective. This is why it's so important to clear out all the aspects of your life that are limiting your ability to go further. In the previous chapters, I discussed ways of healing your wounds, traumas, and life challenges; connecting to yourself and others; and the importance of your connectedness to your body. We explored the activation of certain chemicals and hormones to make you feel better, ultimately all the self-care you need to do to be a fully functioning being. Now that you have a greater understanding of how to do that, you can begin to explore self-actualization and self-transcendence. It's important get to a place where you can feel content and fulfilled in your life. When you arrive at this place, you're more open to exploring yourself further. This is where self-transcendence begins to play a role. People begin to realize there must be more to life; so, the journey of discovery takes on a whole new level. You begin to feel you need to "level up," upscale, and elevate your sense of self. This space is truly beautiful, you begin to feel a greater sense of awareness and expansion. You tap in to emotions of awe, ecstasy, and elevation; you connect with something higher; and you begin to look outside yourself. These states are related to higher performance levels and a greater frequency of peak experiences. Getting there requires dedication, intention, and attention to meeting your needs in the most wholesome ways possible.

It is very hard to contemplate meditating or being in a state of creative flow if you're starving, exhausted, anxious, and in pain. It's almost like expecting your smart phone to work quickly with low battery power and slow Internet connection. If you don't expect this from your phone, why do you expect this from yourself? The mind and body have basic needs and they must be met for higher functioning. If you want to attain higher levels of consciousness and improve your performance, you have to look after yourself. Self-care is investing in yourself so that you can be even more amazing.

Master your ability to create a calm space in your mind. Allow your body to be rested. Nourish your soul with things that are fulfilling. Make space for stillness. Create the right conditions for your well-being in general and for mystical experiences. If your mind is full of anxious thoughts and worries, there is no space for calm and creative thinking. It's that simple. There is no room for an experience of transcendence to occur. The more creativity you can step into, greater sense of humour, acceptance of yourself and life, the greater the feelings of self-actualization. Self-actualize so you can transcend. This sets the stage for a life that feels purposeful, connected, and wholesome; you'll feel content. This space opens you up to explore greater states of awareness. Bliss, awe, and flow enriches your life and makes it sweeter, ultimately creating a life worth living. When life feels this good, you'll seek experiences that take you beyond yourself. Your curiosity will be sparked to begin exploring and expanding your awareness. This is why it's so important to do your healing work and clear the path for you to step into higher states of consciousness.

Transcendence, Flow & Other Beautiful States

A transcendental experience is a spiritual experience that goes beyond the ordinary everyday life experiences. It is characterised as something that goes beyond the self, beyond space and time as you know it. You feel a sense of oneness, there is a sense of awe, a sense that there is something grander to life than just you. You let go of the perception that you are separate from the world. It feels timeless and spaceless, a sense of union with all that is. This could happen to you in meditation, on a hike in nature, immersed in a task, or as you're writing creative thoughts. These experiences increase your sense of well-being and give you a sense of happiness. They create a feeling of achievement and satisfaction in your life, all this while expanding your consciousness.

Mihaly Csikszentmihalyi is one of the greatest contributors in the field of flow, he states that you need to have order and harmony in your consciousness to get to optimal states. You want to chase the experience for the sake of having the experience, not to prove anything to anyone else, just you. This ties in to living your life for you, not to prove anything to anyone. You are having the experience for the pure pleasure of having the experience. You have let go trying to prove anything to anyone; you are you.

Think about your life; what aspects do you feel are in order? Is there harmony in your home? When you feel order and harmony, have you noticed that things flow more easily?

You see, everyone wants to be happy; it is an internal state that cannot be bought. It requires you to feel in alignment with your values, thoughts, feelings, and, most importantly, your actions. When you feel you are in alignment and your life truly represents who you are, you are more likely to go with the flow, be more open, and less pushy and controlling. This allows you to listen to the gentle whispers and cues life gives you. You are allowing, listening, and open to guidance from life. This requires a sense of trust in yourself and in life, trusting that little gut instinct whenever it pops up.

In flow states, your brain undergoes hypofrontality. Here the frontal lobe shuts down its level of activity and allows other areas of the brain to work in greater level of intensity. They begin communicating at higher speeds, allowing a greater level of creativity to be experienced (Csikszentmihalyi, 2008). This creativity is part of the activation of a flow state. When you are experiencing higher levels of creativity, you are more likely to lose your sense of self and self-consciousness. You become so immersed in the task at hand that you lose track of time. These sensations are related to states of bliss, the brain secretes large amounts of chemicals that make you feel good. These experiences ultimately lead you to healing and higher functioning of the brain.

The more you can get in to a state of flow and creativity, the more you can continuously secrete the right type of chemicals. When you begin to realize you can do this with several techniques, you are driving your experiences. Once this happens, you engage with the world in a much more open, excited, and loving manner. You begin to experience richer more loving interactions. You become the designer of your mind, the master of your emotions. Your attention now shifts to actively creating a new reality; you are shaping your brain, your mind, and your life. This allows you to show up to the world in a more open, confident, and positive manner. The world starts to respond to you in much the same way. When you begin to feel the magic of this, you begin to implement more positive coping mechanisms and make time for your mind. By doing this, not only are you improving your ability to regulate your emotions but you feel more capable. It becomes a beautiful self-fulfilling prophecy. You feel better, so you engage with life more confidently; this creates better outcomes, you start believing in yourself more.

These experiences begin to positively shape you. You'll look forward to the day to see what you can explore. Curiosity spikes and you have a thirst for a new experience, wondering what the next blissful experience will be. If you start thinking in this way, you're sending commands to your mind to look for these experiences. This sparks a sense of exhilaration, think how much your life would change if you felt enthusiastic every day. Going out into the world with this sense of excitement activates the playful child parts within you. Every day is seen as a new day to explore, discover, and experience life. This makes life feel lighter.

When this begins to happen, you realize that life is really magical. You might even craft the belief that life is really just a beautiful game to be played. Life turns into a place where imagination has a lead role. A place where flow, bliss, mystical experiences are the norm. You start to look at life with fascination; your priorities change. A sense of exploration now holds a greater value. How much more can you possibly discover? The power you feel when you realize you are constructing these states is nothing short of magnificent. With this mindset, your life begins to change and extraordinary events unfold. You will notice that your brain begins to function more efficiently. Your cognitive abilities will improve, you'll enhance your performance, and you'll start having a sense of "winning." This is truly the embodied experience of empowered minds.

> *"Whatever the mind can conceive and believe,*
> *it can achieve."*
> —Napoleon Hill

Blissful Living

Bliss is a state that people all over the world search for, a state of being in complete happiness, unified with all consciousness and sense of existence. You need peace of mind to access higher states of consciousness. You need peace of mind to access blissful states.

Meditation, altered states of consciousness, can gently open the door to these higher states. Sometimes, when you let go, there is a soft surrender that propels you into a state of bliss.

With death comes rebirth; one day ends and gives light to the next. This is the cycle of life. We are forever being born again with new ideas, new concepts, ever-changing transformations. Be aware of your existence and recognize you are pure consciousness, everlasting and forever evolving. When you act, be clear, have intent, and do so with grace and confidence; otherwise, just don't act at all. Act with effortless grace, move with confidence, feel with the heart. If you dare not love fully, why live at all? Love with all you've got; there is nothing to lose. You may not be loved in return, but you have loved nevertheless. To feel hurt is to feel alive; to not love is to not live.

There is no beginning and no end in awareness of who you are; it is an ever-evolving cycle that allows your existence to be graced by bliss. When you become aware of yourself, let the awareness illuminate your being like luminous creatures deep in the ocean. Be the light that shows the way; don't wait for the perfect situation, go with your flow. When you allow stillness and silence to be your companions, you gently allow bliss to be tasted. Let bliss be part of your essence; spread your essence through the world like gentle winds of the south.

Fill your heart not with hatred and rumination, for it will poison your essence; instead, fill it with harmony, love, and tranquillity. It is beautiful to have a tranquil heart, one that can grow with the passion of life when stimulated and can gently calm your sleeping soul to rest. Speak gently to your elders as you hold their supple hands and listen to the stories that created the world you now live in. Be one with them. Honor their journey; hold them in harmony, for you will be old one day too.

*"I cannot make you understand. I cannot understand what
is happening inside me. I cannot even explain it to myself"*
—Franz Kafka, *The Metamorphosis*

Exercise

- Put 528hz music, theta sound or gentle relaxing music on.
- Close your eyes.
- Create the intention of having a beautiful experience.
- Imagine you begin to breathe in light, fill your body with light.
- Start with your lungs, let it spread to your heart, your abdomen, your other organs. Imagine the light spreading through up and down your spine all the way to the tips of your fingers from head to toe.
- Allow every breath to fill your body, relax your mind.
- Now imagine floating out of your body covered in a cocoon of light. Float up toward the sky and allow yourself to notice beautiful lights of all colors and warmth. Feel yourself held safely in your cocoon of white light. Allow yourself to float and expand.
- Feel held in white light, imagine a sense of floating freedom, held by this light. Gently let go of tension in your muscles, letting go slowly with every breath, letting go of the perception of your body.
- Imagine turning into pure white light. Every part of you turns to light, vibrating at the frequency of pure light. Imagine your consciousness expanding and, as you do, you allow your awareness to expand. Feel a sense of freedom and liberation in doing this. Imagine you are

pure consciousness in the form of light, and, as you do this, allow yourself to just be.

- Enjoy the feeling of expansive consciousness, freedom, and unlimited awareness. Fill your awareness with unconditional love and unlimited joy. Feel your awareness expanding with peace and tranquillity. Allow those feelings to just float in your awareness.

- As you do this, allow yourself to have this sensation however it unfolds.

- Slowly bring your awareness of your body back into your perception. As you do, use your imagination and fill every particle, cell, muscle, and fibre of your being with this magnificent sense of love and joy. You are programming and putting yourself together with a pattern of unconditional love and joy. Every part of your being receives this openly. Every cell in your body, every thought, every feeling is now imbued with this magical energy of love and joy. Feel it just gently flowing around and within you. It is part of you.

- Gently begin to float back down into your body. Bring your awareness into your body. Take a moment to imagine your body is shining and glowing with this light. It is the pure magnificent energy of unconditional love and joy; your entire being is glowing. This energy now forms a part of your conscious awareness.

- Take a deep breath and open your eyes, coming back fully to the present moment.

This exercise is such a beautiful way of allowing your consciousness to expand. Imagine you let go of your body, freeing yourself from the constraints of the physicality. You float, you expand, you move through space and time. You allow yourself to have an experience of you as pure energy.

Then, when you're ready to come back into your body, you program it to be filled with unconditional love and joy. As you do this and you practice, you will soon notice you can easily flow in and out of states of meditative awareness. You will flow in and out of states of altered consciousness. Sometimes, you might feel a tingling sensation; sometimes, you might experience a lapse in time. All of these sensations are different ways of expanding your consciousness. It goes beyond the normal daily activity of the brain. It is novel and different to daily experiences. Your mind will ebb and flow from attention to wandering off; that is perfectly normal.

The more you get use to the experience of expanding your consciousness, floating, and letting go, the more you can begin to train your mind. You will become more comfortable and familiar with the idea of expanding. Becoming more than the limited perception of you as your body.

CONCLUSION

Blissful Words To Send You Off On A Wonderful
Journey With An Empowered Mind.

You will eventually arrive home, to YOU. When this happens, you will realize many things. You will notice you are pure conscious awareness, energy, cosmic and powerful beyond belief, filled with the ability to create any state you desire. You have been gifted with the most magnificent qualities; use them. These qualities, if used wisely, will propel you into realms within your consciousness that will astound you. You will begin to truly believe in yourself. When you do this, get ready. Get ready for your life to blossom, your health to improve, and miracles to unfold. Life is a miracle; just think long enough about it and you too will realize this.

You will expand; this is a growth process. It may hurt at times; it may feel uncomfortable. Remind yourself you are expanding. Do so with love. In this process of expansion, you may even feel your potential, unlimited life force filled with everlasting possibilities.

You may even transform and become luminous with radiance. You will keep expanding, growing, becoming better and more magnificent every day. When you crumble, you will gently pick yourself back up and lovingly put yourself together. You will realize that crumbling is part of the process; you will embrace it and accept it as it is. Your love will grow and your heart will expand. Your unlimited nature will show you the way to feeling that all life is love. You will expand a little more, a little more empowered and sure of yourself. In this journey, you will continue to evolve, expanding, noticing you are light energy. The light just continues to be light; there is no beginning and no end; it just is. Is this the secret of life?

THANK YOU

Thank you for purchasing this book, I hope you have enjoyed it and feel inspired. If this book has moved you to feel more empowered, share it and gift it. Let's create a worldwide ripple effect of empowerment.

I'd love to hear from you, please leave a review online. If you'd like to access more hypnotic meditations please go to: https://alfapsychology.com/products/

Visit Kali's website to access personalized sessions to empower your mind, online training and resources www.alfapsychology.com

The ladybug has been chosen as the spirit animal for this book. She is a symbol of good luck, profound transformation, and divine intervention. Ladybug also represents graceful transitions and pure love, may you be blessed with all these wonderful aspects on your journey.

ABOUT THE AUTHOR

Kalí Alfaro is a Psychologist and Hypnotherapist based in Perth, Australia. Kalí was born in Chile and migrated to Australia as a young child. Kalí is a humanitarian, an Earth keeper and lover of nature. Kalí's fascination with the human mind, heart and conscious evolution has driven her desire to explore healing modalities and the world. Her passion to help people connect to their true self is her driving force.

She holds a Master in Psychology with an emphasis on Health, a Bachelor of Communications, and has received numerous postgraduate training in Hypnosis. She has traveled the world learning traditional and ancient healing modalities for the last twenty years. Moved by the mystery of ancient cultures and healing aspects of nature, she is constantly feeding her nomadic nature to explore, continue learning, and experience life. Kalí has worked as a Psychologist in remote indigenous communities, hospital settings, government departments and has consulted with organizations.

She currently runs a private Psychology practice, group retreats, and online well-being forums. She is available for workshops, retreats, and guest speaker events. Kalí can be found online at www.kalialfaro.com and www.alfapsychology.com

REFERENCES

Bauer, R. (2019). Ontology of bliss: A phenomenology. *Revista Científica Arbitrada de la Fundación MenteClara, 4* (2), 55-70.

Brannan, D., Davis, A., & Biswas-Diener, R. (2016). *The science of forgiveness, examining the influence of forgiveness on mental health.* Elsevier.

Carter, S. C., & Progres, S. W. (2013). The biochemistry of love: An oxytocin hypothesis. *The European Molecular Biology Organization 14*(1) 12-16.

Csikszentmihalyi, M. (2008). *Flow. The psychology of optimal experiences.* Harper Collins.

Danese, A., & Lewis, S. J. (2017). Psychoneuroimmonology of early life stress: The hidden wounds of childhood trauma? *Neuropsychopharmacology 42,* 99-114.

Darwin, C. (1872). *The expression of emotions in man & animals.*

Esch, T., & Stefano, G. B. (2005). The neurobiology of love. *Neuroendocrinology Letters* (26) 175-192.

Esch, T. (2103). *The neurobiology of meditation & mindfulness.* Neuroscience Research Institute.

Einstein, A. (2007). *The world as I see it.* BN Publishing

Fisch, S., Brinkhaus, B., & Teut, M. (2017). Hypnosis in patients with perceived stress–A systemic review. *BMC Complementary and Alternative Medicine, 17,* 323

Hansen, C. J., Stevens, L. C., & Coast, J. R. (2001). Exercise duration and mood state: How much is enough to feel better? *Journal of Health Psychology* (20), 267-275.

Jung, C. (1963). *Memories, dreams, reflections. An autobiography.* William Collins.

Lane, A. M., & Lovejoy, D. J. (2001). The effects of exercise on mood changes: The moderating effect of depressed mood. *Journal of Sports Medicine and Physical Fitness, 2001*(41), 539-545

Leuchter, A. F., Cook, I. A., Witte, E. A., Morgan, M., & Abrams, M. (2002). Changes in brain function of depressed subjects during treatment with placebo. *American Journal of Psychiatry 159*(1), 122-129.

Li, Q. (2018). *Into the forest. How trees can help you find health and happiness.* Penguin Random House.

Lipton, B. (2016). *The biology of belief: Unleashing the power of consciousness, matter & miracles.* Hay House.

Ludwig, A. M., & Levine, J. (1965). Alterations in consciousness produced by hypnosis. *Journal of Nervous & Mental Diseases, 140* (2), 146-153.

Mandela, N. (1994). *Long walk to freedom.* Abacus.

McCall, T. (2007). *Yoga as medicine. The yogic prescription for health & healing.* Bantam Dell.

Moorjani, A. (2012). *Dying to be me: My journey from cancer to near death, to healing.* Hay House.

Nelson-Isaacs, S. (2019). *Living in Flow: The science of synchronicity and how your choices shape your world.* North Atlantic Books.

Nussbaum, M. (2016). *Anger & forgiveness.* Oxford University Press.

Pert, C. B. (1997). *Molecules of emotions: Why you feel the way you feel.* Simon &Schuster.

Ricciardi, E., Rota, G., Sani, Lorenzo, G. C., Gaglianese, A., Gauzelli, M., & Pietrini, P. (2013). How the brain heals emotional wounds: The functional neuroanatomy of forgiveness. *Frontiers in Human Neuroscience,* (7), 839.

Rossi, E. (2007). Shen psycho-emotional aspects of Chinese medicine. Churchill Livingstone, Elsevier.

Segerstrom, S. C., & Miller, G. E. (2004). Psychological stress and the human immune system: A meta analytic study of 30 years of inquiry. *Psychological Bulletin, 130*(4), 601-630.

Scovel Shinn, F. (1989). *The wisdom of Florence Scovel Shinn. 4 complete books, The game of life, The power of the spoken word, Your word is your wand, The secret of success.* Amazon.

Srinivasan, V., Smits, M., Spence, W., Lowe, A. D, Kayumov, L., Pandi-Perumal, S. R., Parry, B., & Cardinali, D. P. (2009). Melatonin in mood disorders. *The World Journal of Biological Psychiatry,* (7) 138-151.

Szabo, A. (2003). The acute effects of humor and exercise on mood and anxiety, *Journal of Leisure Research,* (35) 152-162.

Toussaint, L., Shields, G., Dorn, G., & Slavich, G. (2016). Effects of lifetime stress exposure on mental and physical health in young adulthood: How stress degrades and forgiveness protects health. *Journal of Health Psychology, 21*(6), 1004-1014.

Vaitl, D., Birbaumer, N., Gruzelier, J., Jamieson, G., Kotchoubey, B., Kübler, A., Lehmann, D., Miltner, W. H. R., Ott, U., Pütz, P., Sammer, G., Strauch, I., Strehl, U., Wackermann,

J., & Weiss, T. (2005). Psychobiology of altered states of consciousness. *Psychological Bulletin, 131*(1), 98–127.

Vanhaudenhuyse, A., Laureys, S., & Faymonville, M. E. (2014). Neurophysiology of hypnosis. *Clinical Neurophysiology, 44*(4), 343-353.

Walsch, N. D. (1996). *Conversations with God.* Hampton Roads.

Weiss, B. L. (1988). *Many lives many masters: The true story of a prominent psychiatrist, his young patient, and the past-life therapy that changed both their lives.* Simon & Schuster.

Weitsenhoffer, A (1989). *The practice of hypnotism Vol 1 & 2.* John Wiley & Sons.

Worthington, E. L., vanOyen W. C., Lerner, A. J., & Scherer, M. (2005). Forgiveness in health research and medical practice. *Explore 1*(3), 169-176.

Zelinka, V. (2014). Hypnosis, attachment and oxytocin: An integrative perspective. *International Journal of Clinical and Experimental Hypnosis, 62*(1), 29-49.

Made in the USA
Middletown, DE
28 May 2021